The International Collectors' Guide to
Cigarette

with Values

Dr. Fernando Righini & Marco Papazzoni

4880 Lower Valley Road, Atglen, PA 19310 USA

Designed by Dr. Fernando Righini & Marco Papazzoni

ISBN: 0-7643-0448-8
Printed in the United States of America
1 2 3 4

Published by Schiffer Publishing Ltd.
4880 Lower Valley Road
Atglen, PA 19310
Phone: (610) 593-1777; Fax: (610) 593-2002
E-mail: Schifferbk@aol.com
Please write for a free catalog.
This book may be purchased from the publisher.
Please include $3.95 for shipping.

Please try your bookstore first.

We are interested in hearing from authors
with book ideas on related subjects.

Preface

Cigarette pack collection belongs to the area of so-called "minor" collecting. It is "Minor" because, although these collectors are to be found around the world, there are only a few tens of thousands of them. What the group lacks in size, they make up in experience and organization, above all in the USA, Great Britain, South America and Japan.

There are probably two main reasons which have led so many people to collect cigarette packs and boxes. First of all, cigarette packs, especially the older styles, are often very beautiful and beautifully made, and are thus both fascinating and attractive in themselves. The second reason, less obvious but perhaps the more profound of the two, is that this is an area in which, in the absence of catalogues, rules and official valuations, the collector is free to follow his whimsy and passion wherever it leads him. To be a cigarette pack collector, it is not enough to enter a specialist shop with money in your pocket and buy the items you desire, as so often happens in stamp collecting; it requires talent, patience, skill and tenacity to track down a rare piece, often following the most unlikely clues to their conclusion.

There is no greater satisfaction than finally to hold in your hands a rare and beautiful cigarette pack after weeks and even months of patient searching.

Introduction

A Short History of Tobacco and Cigarettes

Tobacco has a recent history and we are still able to relive the occasion on which it became known to western civilization.

I quote here from *Historias de las Indias,* written by Father Bartolomeo de las Casas, a companion of Christopher Columbus. The two "Christians" mentioned in the account are Luis de Torres and Rodrigo de Jeres di Ajamonte, members of Columbus's crew.

Island of Cuba, November 2nd, 1492
"These two Christians in their travels met many people going from village to village, both men and women with a glowing coal in one hand and certain herbs, in order to savor their perfume, these herbs being dried and wrapped in a dried leaf in the form of a tube ... lit at one end..."

In little more than a century the tobacco plant spread throughout the world thanks to its adaptability to all climates and terrains. The custom of smoking tobacco spread equally quickly among the people without distinction of social class, to the extent that the tax on tobacco soon became one of the principal sources of income for governments.

In the 17th and 18th centuries tobacco was smoked mainly in pipes or taken as snuff, while the cigar came to dominate only in the next century.

The first documented account of cigarettes comes to us from 1739, in the Spanish "Diccionario de autoridades" in which it is explained how the chopped leaves of the tobacco plant can be smoked in "cigarros de papel" (paper wrapped cigars), rather than wrapped in whole leaves of the plant. In reality these first "cigarillos" were generally smoked by poorer people who made use of discarded stubs and the remains of the chopped leaves wrapped in paper, being unable to afford the more expensive leaf-wrapped cigars.

Cigarette production is mentioned in France in 1843 and during the Crimean War in 1854, although only in passing. Manual large-scale production started in 1856-60 in France, Russia and England.

Up to the end of the 19th century the cigarette was considered a variant of the cigar, often as a feminine article. It was only in the First World War that the cigarette became an article of mass appeal, growing to account for its present 90% of tobacco consumption.

Collecting

The Pack

While there are no rigid rules, the object of cigarette pack collecting is the pack itself, of whatever type, paper, cardboard, metal or plastic. The following types are known:

- ✧ the paper pack
- ✧ the cardboard envelope
- ✧ the cardboard pack (Flip-top), occasionally made of plastic
- ✧ the drawer-type cardboard box (Hull and Slide)
- ✧ the cardboard box (Box), occasionally made of plastic
- ✧ the metal box (Tin)
- ✧ the fabric wrapper

Some collectors prefer to collect the entire pack, sealed with the original cigarettes inside, while others open them up to spread out the pack (this also simplifies filing). As a rule it is preferable to preserve the pack in its original form, especially boxes and tins, as this best displays their aesthetic qualities. Many collectors refurbish their most interesting pieces.

Storage

There are no special containers for cigarette packs. The whole packs and boxes are usually stored on shelves or in showcases, always in dry, well-ventilated atmospheres to prevent damaging mold-formation and condensation. Sealed containers are therefore unsuitable. The opened or spread-out packs can be stored in file boxes or albums, although the former are preferable due to the variation in thickness of the packs. It is better not to cut the pieces in any way for easier storage; many collectors will refuse cut pieces.

Values

It is clear that this aspect must also be evaluated with reference to the preceding parameters.

- ✧ Cigarette tins. These deserve separate treatment, since there are many collectors of lithograph tin containers in general who therefore widen the market enormously. It is thus relatively easy to find tin cigarette boxes, but their value is usually much greater than that of the simple cigarette pack. Prices range from about $5 for the most common and baldly preserved items to $500 for the rarest, most beautiful pieces in the best condition. It is important to realize that the value of a box may vary from $10 to $150 according to its condition.

The following values are approximate and do not take into account the period of currency of the pack:

- ✧ Common pack: from 30 cents to $3 according to condition, rarity, nationality etc. From $2 to $5 if the article is complete.
- ✧ Uncommon packs: from $1 to $20. $5 to $50 if complete.
- ✧ Rare packs: $5 to $50. More if complete.
- ✧ Very rare packs: $20 and up.
- ✧ Extremely rare packs: $40 and up.

- ✧ Conclusions. One thing emerges very clearly from the above considerations: the value of a cigarette pack can vary enormously according how much the seller wants to sell and the buyer, for his part, to buy. For example a Brazilian collector can buy an English pack at the flea market for $1 and sell it on to an English collector for $30, who will, in turn, realize $60 selling it in a specialty auction.

Further information

The three principal clubs of cigarette pack collectors; they also publish specialist magazines:

USA : C.P.C.A,
61 Searle Street,
Georgetown, MA 01833

Great Britain : C.P.C.A., Roy & Nuala Gilbert,
Warden's Flat,
Nuffield College,
Lincoln's Inn Fields,
London WC2A 3PN

Brazil : Associaçao dos Colecionadores de
Embalagens de Cigarros,
Caixa Postal 5264,
Centro Cep 01061,
Sao Paulo, SP

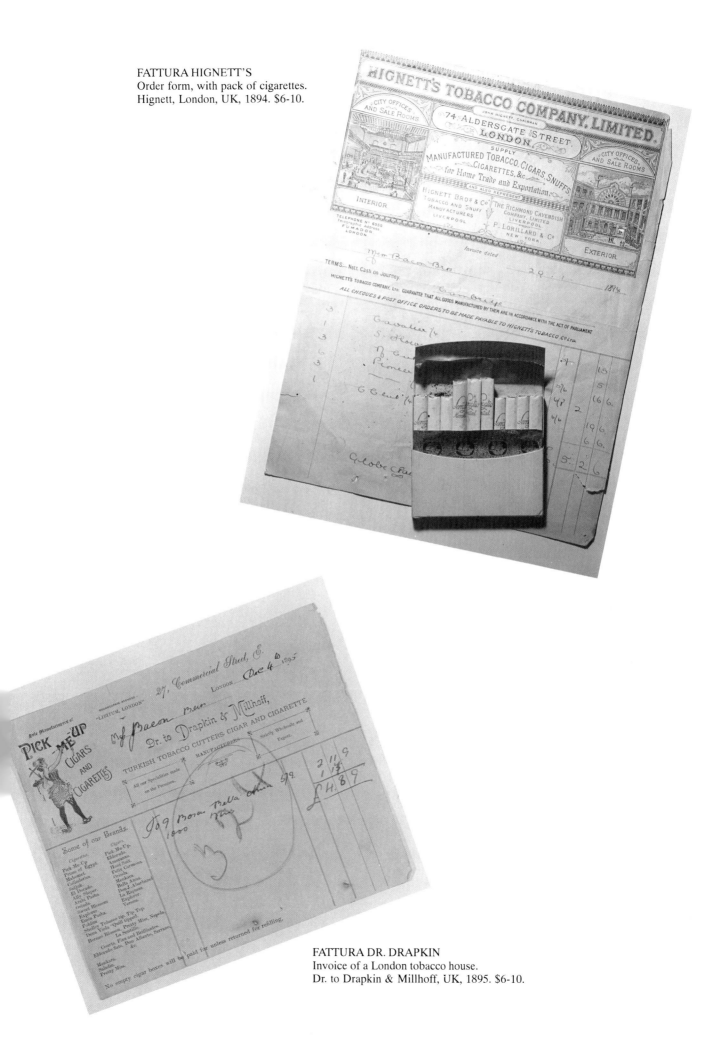

FATTURA HIGNETT'S
Order form, with pack of cigarettes.
Hignett, London, UK, 1894. $6-10.

FATTURA DR. DRAPKIN
Invoice of a London tobacco house.
Dr. to Drapkin & Millhoff, UK, 1895. $6-10.

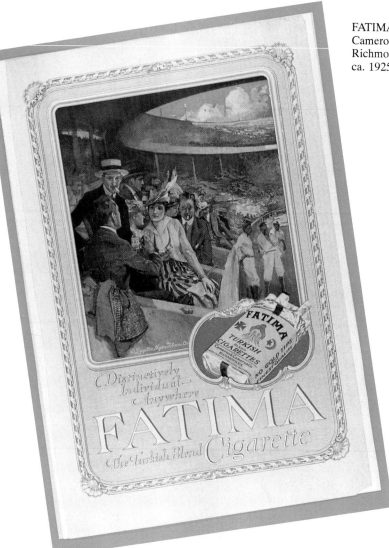

FATIMA ADVERTISEMENT
Cameron & Cameron Co.,
Richmond, VA, USA,
ca. 1925. $6-10

LUCKY STRIKE BRIDGE GAMES
The American Tob. Co, NC,
USA, ca. 1925. $6-10.

SEITANES POSTCARD
Seita, France, ca. 1980. $1-5.

REDFORD NAVY CUT ADVERTISEMENT
Redford & Co., London, UK, ca. 1900. $1-5

A-A GUN - 10 cig.
Chuan Hin Tob. Factory
Pakistan, ca. 1950. $6-10.

BDULLA No. 11 TURKISH - 20 cig.
bdulla & Co Ltd., London - UK
1. 1935. Tin, $6-10.

ABDULLA No. 16 - 50 cig.
Abdulla & Co., London - UK
ca. 1925. $11-20.

ABDULLA TURCOS - 20 cig.
Abdulla & Co., Ltd., London, UK,
ca. 1960. $6-10.

BDULLA - 25 cig.
dulla & Co. London - UK, ca. 1960. $6-10.

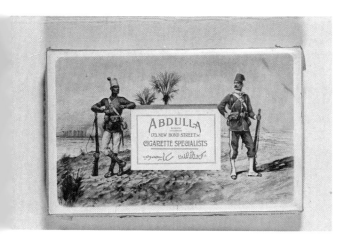

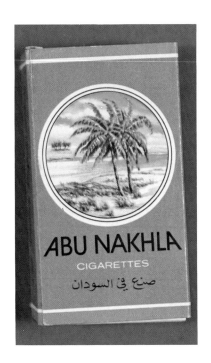

AGUILAS - 20 cig.
El Aguila SA,
Santa Cruz, Mexico,
ca. 1960. $1-5.

ABDULLA FILTRE - 20 cig.
Abdulla & Co., Ltd., London, UK, ca. 1965. $1-5.

ABU NAKLA - 10 cig.
Saudi Arabia, ca. 1970. $1-5.

AIDE DE CAMP - 50 cig.
Westminster Tob. Co., London, UK, ca. 1938. $6-10.

ALBANA - 20 cig.
Orienta SA Lugano,
Switzerland, ca. 1940. $6-10.

AKBAR SHAH - 10 cig.
Imperial Tob. Co., India,
ca. 1950. $6-10.

ALL JACKS - 20 cig.
C. Peper Tob. Co., USA,
ca. 1950. $11-20.

ALFA ROMEO - 10 cig.
Monopoli di Stato,
Italy, ca. 1960. $11-20.

ALBATROS - 20 cig.
Made in Poland, ca. 1965. $1-5.

ALMA MATER
Bacon Bros, Cambridge, UK
ca. 1900. $6-10.

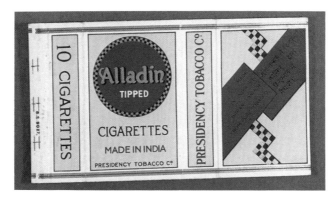

ALLADIN - 10 cig.
Presidency Tob. Co., India,
ca. 1950. $6-10.

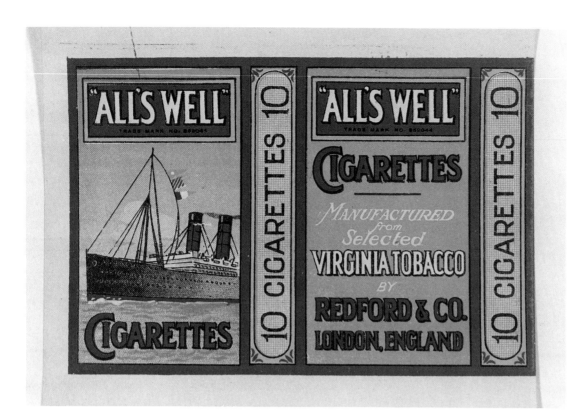

ALL'S WELL - 10 cig.
Redford & Co., London, U[
ca. 1910. $11-20.

AMERICAN SPIRIT - 20 cig.
T.P. 25, NY, USA,
ca. 1975. $1-5.

AMERICAN CLUB EXPORT - 2
Sullana Ltd., Zurich, Switzerland
ca. 1965. $1-5.

AMOROSA - 20 cig.
R. Pansieri, Alger, Algeria,
ca. 1950. $6-10.

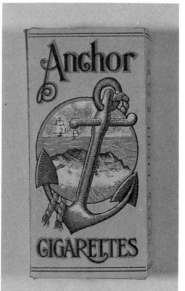

ANCHOR - 8 cig.
Made in Trinidad, ca. 1928.
$11-20.

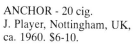
ANCHOR - 20 cig.
J. Player, Nottingham, UK,
ca. 1960. $6-10.

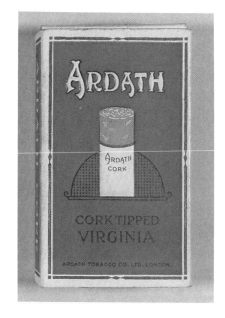

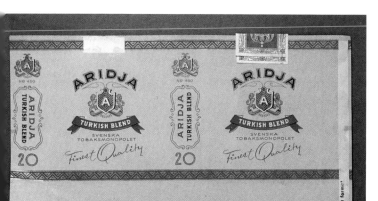

ARIDJA - 20 cig.
Svenska Tobaks
Monopolet,
Sweden, ca. 1950.
$1-5.

ARDATH CORK - 10 cig.
Ardath Tob. Co., London,
UK, ca. 1930. $6-10.

ARK ROYAL - 50 cig.
The Premier Tob., London, UK,
ca. 1950. $11-20.

ANSTIE'S MILD - 10 cig.
E. & V. Anstie Ltd., Devizes,
UK, ca. 1930. $1-5.

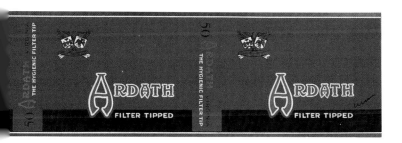

ARDATH FILTER TIPPED - 50 cig.
Ardath Tob. Co., London, UK, ca. 1950. $6-10.

ARDATH PLAIN - 20 cig.
Ardath Tob. Co., UK
ca. 1950. $6-10.

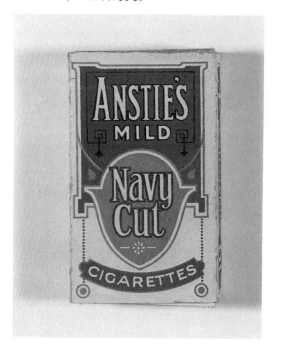

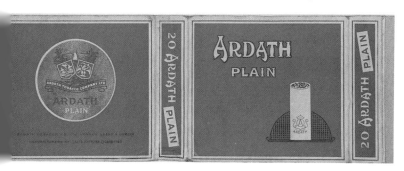

APOLLO SOYUZ - 20 cig.
Yava Factory, Moscow,
USSR, ca. 1975. $1-5.

ARAKS - 20 cig.
Tchamkerten Anvers, Holland,
ca. 1955. $1-5.

ANDRON - 10 cig.
Georgopulo New York, NY,
USA, ca. 1960. $1-5.

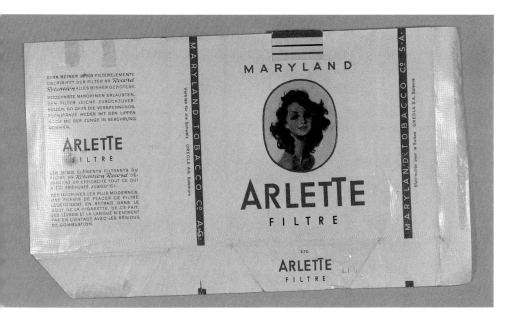

ARLETTE - 20 cig.
Maryland Tob. Co. AG,
Switzerland, ca. 1975. $1-5.

ARISTOCRATIC - 10 cig.
C. Colombos Ltd., Egypt,
ca. 1920. $6-10.

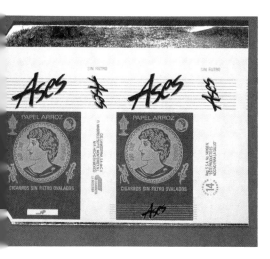

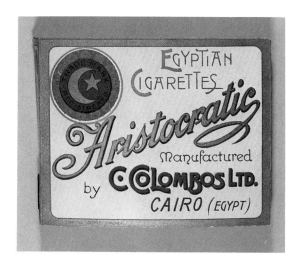

ASES - 14 cig.
Cigarrera La Moderna, Mexico,
ca. 1980. $1-5.

ATHLETE - 20 cig.
D. Ritchie & Co., Montreal, Canada,
ca. 1890. $21-40.

ARISTOCRATIC - 20 cig.
C. Colombos Ltd., Egypt,
ca. 1920. $6-10.

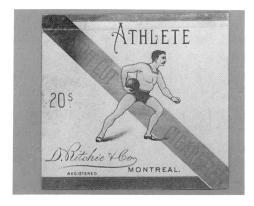

ASIA - 20 cig.
Iranian Tob. Co.,
Iran, ca. 1969. $6-10.

ARAKS MYLORD - 25 cig.
Tchamkerten & Co., Anvers,
Holland, ca. 1930. Tin, $11-20.

ARIZONA - 20 cig.
Made in Holland
ca. 1950. $1-5.

ARMY CLUB - 50 cig.
G. Phillips London, UK, ca. 1945. Tin, $11-20.

ARMADA - 3 cig.
Made in Holland,
ca. 1960. $1-5.

ARMY CLUB - 10 cig.
Cavanders Ltd., London,
UK, ca. 1940. $1-5.

Atos - 20 cig.
Atos Gmbh, Germany,
ca. 1955. Tin, $11-20.

AUTO SEDAN - 20 cig.
T Nojorono, Kudus, Indonesia, ca. 1980. $1-5.

ATIKAH - 12 cig.
Delta, Dresden, Germany,
ca. 1925. $11-20.

IZ - 20 cig.
a Portuguesa de Tabacos,
tugal, ca. 1955. $1-5.

B.B. Cigarettes - 20 cig.
Bacon Bros, Cambridge, UK,
ca. 1900. $6-10.

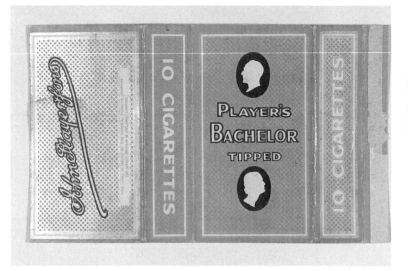

BACHELOR TIPPED - 10 cig.
J. Player, Nottingham, UK,
ca. 1950. $6-10.

BACON BROS
Bacon Bros, Cambridge, UK,
ca. 1900. $6-10.

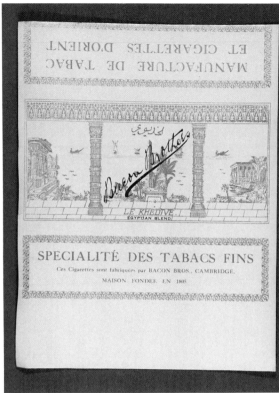

BACHELOR CORK TIPS - 20 cig.
J. Player, Nottingham, UK, ca. 1950. $6-10.

BACON'S GOLD FLAKE - 100 cig.
Bacon Bros, Cambridge, UK, ca. 1910. $6-10.

BACON'S GOLD FLAKE - 50 cig.
Bacon Bros, Cambridge, UK,
ca. 1910. $6-10.

BALCANA - 20 cig.
Lario SA, Chiasso,
Switzerland,
ca. 1930. $1-5.

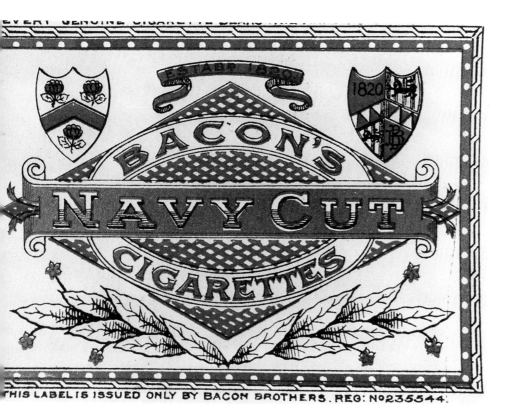

BACON'S NAVY CUT
Bacon Bros, Cambridge, UK,
ca. 1910. $6-10.

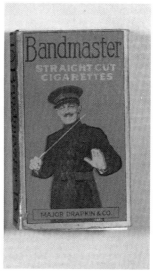

BANDMASTER - 10 cig.
Major Drapkin & Co., London,
UK, ca. 1940. $11-20.

BALTO - 50 cig.
Seita, France, ca. 1938. Tin, $11-20.

BALLERINA - 20 cig.
Made in Belgium,
ca. 1960. $1-5.

BAR ONE - 10 cig.
J. Wix & Sons, London,
UK, ca. 1950. $6-10.

BANGLE - 20 cig.
U.L. Allen Ginter, Richmond, Va.,
Holland, ca. 1965. $1-5.

BEAR'S NUMBER ONE - 50 cig.
Thomas Bear & Sons, London, UK,
ca. 1930. $6-10.

BALINTAWAK - 30 cig.
Bataan Cig. & Cig. Fact. Quezon City,
Philippines, ca. 1965. $1-5.

BEAR'S SPECIALS - 50 cig.
Thomas Bear & Sons, London-India, ca. 1935. $6-10.

BEE CIGARETTES - 20 cig.
Sampoerna Cig. Co. Ltd.,
Indonesia, ca. 1960. $1-5.

BEARS' HONEY DEW - 10 cig.
Thomas Bear & Sons, London,
UK, ca. 1950. $1-5.

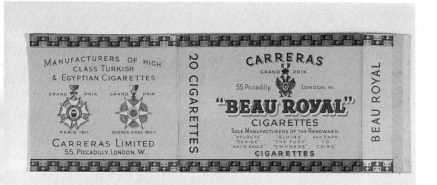

BEAU ROYAL - 20 cig.
Carreras Ltd., London, UK, ca. 1940. $6-10.

BEECHWOOD - 10 cig.
CWS Ltd., Manchester, UK,
ca. 1925. $6-10.

BEER BYSANZ - 20 cig.
Beer, Zurich, Switzerland,
ca. 1932. $11-20.

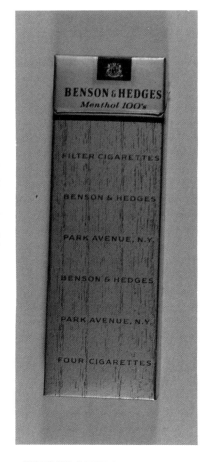

BENSON & HEDGES - 20 cig
B & H, VA - USA
ca. 1965. $1-5.

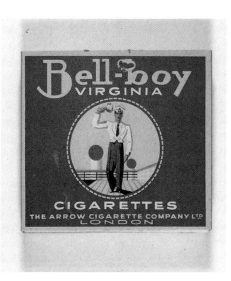

BELL BOY - 20 cig.
The Arrow Cig. Co, London, UK,
ca. 1950. $11-20.

BELWEDER - 20 cig.
WWT, Poznan, Poland,
ca. 1950. $6-10.

BENFICA - 20 cig.
A. Tabaqueria, Portugal, ca. 1965. $1-5.

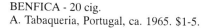

BENSON & HEDGES (top left) - 20 cig.
Benson & Hedges, London, UK,
ca. 1960. Tin for Air France, $11-20.

BENSON & HEDGES (top right) - 20 cig.
Benson & Hedges, London, UK,
ca. 1960. Tin for BEA, $11-20.

BENSON & HEDGES (bottom left) - 20 cig.
Benson & Hedges, London, UK,
ca. 1960. Tin for Alitalia, $11-20.

BENSON & HEDGES (bottom right) - 20 cig.
Benson & Hedges, London, UK,
ca. 1960. Tin for Sabena $11-20.

BISON - 20 cig.
BAT Indonesia,
ca. 1965. $1-5.

BENSON &
HEDGES ACAD-
EMY - 20 cig.
Benson & Hedges,
London, UK, ca.
1975. $1-5.

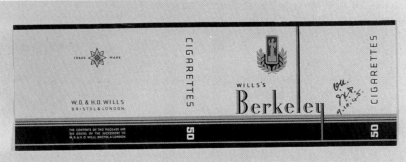

BERKELEY - 50 cig.
W.D. & H.O. Wills, Bristol, UK,
ca. 1935. $6-10.

BENSON & HEDGE
MENTHOL - 4 cig.
Benson & Hedges,
Richmond, Va., USA,
ca. 1975. $6-10.

BISONTE - 20 cig.
Tsabacalera SA, Spain,
ca. 1960. $1-5.

BLACK & RED - 5 cig.
Regie des Tabacs, Monaco,
ca. 1970. $1-5.

BLACK CAT - 50 cig.
Carreras Ltd., Canada,
ca. 1950. Tin, $11-20.

BLACK & WHITE
20 cig.
Marcovitch of Piccadilly,
UK, ca. 1965. $1-5.

BLACK & WHITE LONG SIZE - 20 cig.
Marcovitch of Piccadilly, UK,
ca. 1960. $1-5.

BLACK DEATH - 20 cig.
Black Death Ltd., Cal.,
USA, ca. 1985. $1-5.

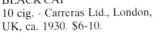

BLACK CAT
10 cig. - Carreras Ltd., London,
UK, ca. 1930. $6-10.

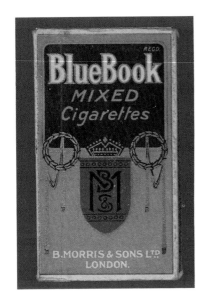

BLUE BOOK - 10 cig.
B. Morris & Sons, London,
UK, ca. 1930. $11-20.

BLUE WAY - 20 cig.
Seita, France, ca. 1980. $1-5.

BOULE D'OR - 12 cig.
Odon Warland, Brussels,
Belgium, ca. 1940. $1-5.

BOGADIR - 25 cig.
Yava, Moscow, USSR,
ca. 1960. $6-10.

BOA VIAGEM - 20 cig.
Emp. Madeirense, Madei
Portugal, ca. 1950. $6-10

BONNE BOUCHE - 50 cig.
Taylor & Breeden, Manchester, UK,
ca. 1920. $21-40.

BRISTOL - 50 cig.
Wills, Bristol, UK, ca. 1935. $11-20.

BRITISH CONSOLS PLAIN ENDS - 25 cig.
MacDonald Tob. Inc., Montreal, Canada, ca. 1960. $1-5.

BROADWAY - 20 cig.
Made in Holland,
ca. 1950. $1-5.

RITISH CONSOLS - 25 cig.
lacDonald Inc, Montreal,
anada, ca. 1944. $11-20.

RISTOL - 50 cig.
V.D. & H.O. Wills, Bristol, UK,
a. 1950. $6-10.

BUFFALO - 20 cig.
C.ia de Cigarros Sinimbu,
Brazil, ca. 1965. $1-5.

BRIDGE CLUB - 20 cig.
Made in Holland,
ca. 1950. $1-5.

BROADWAY - 20 cig.
Maryland Virginia Tob., NY, Switzerland, ca. 1965. $1-5.

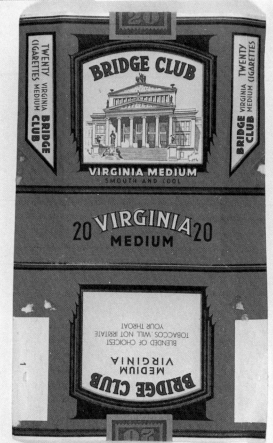

BULGARIA CROWN - 10 cig.
Bulgaria Zig., Dresden, Germany,
ca. 1931. $6-10.

CALENDAR GIRL - 20 cig.
Fact. no. 14, Canada,
ca. 1962. $6-10.

CAMEL - 50 cig.
R.J. Reynolds, NC, USA,
ca. 1950. Tin, $11-20.

BROADWAY - 20 cig.
Maryland Virginia Tob. Co. NY, Switzerland, ca. 1960. $1-5.

CABINET - 100 cig.
F. Syrowatka, Germany,
ca. 1925. Tin, $11-20.

CAFE DE FIRENZE - 10 cig.
Made in Japan,
ca. 1965. $1-5.

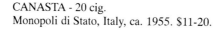

CANASTA - 20 cig.
Monopoli di Stato, Italy, ca. 1955. $11-20.

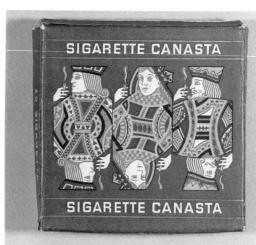

CAMEL - 4 cig.
R.J. Reynolds Tob. Co., USA,
ca. 1960. $6-10.

CANASTA - 20 cig.
Monopoli di Stato, Italy,
ca. 1955. $6-10.

CANEY - 20 cig.
Cubatabaco, Cuba,
ca. 1970. $1-5.

CANASTA - 20 cig.
Monopoli di Stato,
Italy, ca. 1955. $21-40.

CAPITOL - 10 cig.
Made in Malta,
ca. 1930. $1-5.

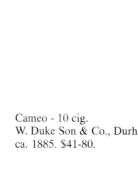

Cameo - 10 cig.
W. Duke Son & Co., Durham NC, USA,
ca. 1885. $41-80.

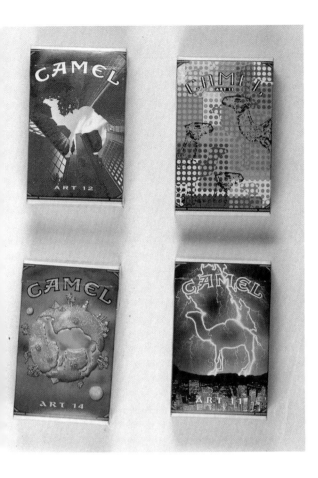

CAMEL ART SELECTION - 20 cig.
R.J. Reynolds, Winston-Salem, USA, ca. 1990. $1-5.

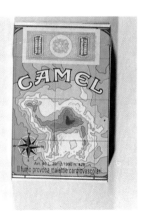

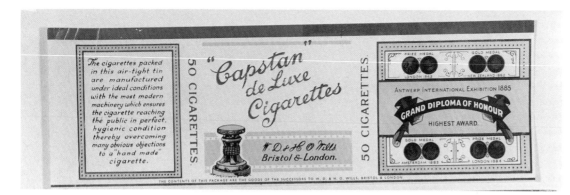

CAPSTAN DE LUXE - 50 ci...
W.D. & H.O. Wills, Bristol,
ca. 1925. $6-10.

CAPSTAN MAGNUMS - 50 cig.
W.D. & H.O. Wills, Bristol,
UK, ca. 1930. $6-10.

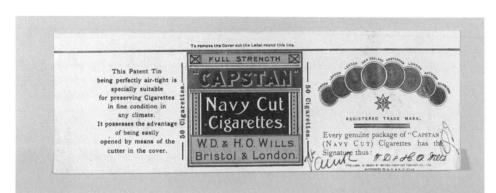

CAPSTAN NAVY CUT FULL - 50 cig.
Wills, Bristol, UK,
ca. 1930 ca. $6-10.

CAPSTAN - 50 cig.
W.D. & H.O. Wills, Bristol, UK, ca. 1950. $11-20.

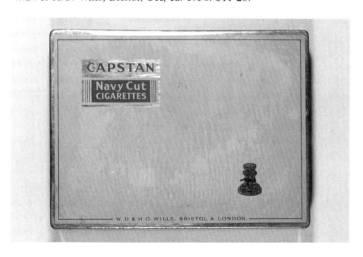

CAPSTAN NAVY CUT MEDIUM - 20 cig.
W.D. & H.O. Wills, Bristol, UK, ca. 1935-ca. $1-5.

CAPSTAN NAVY CUT MEDIUM - 50 cig.
W.D. & H.O. Wills, Bristol, UK, ca. 1940. $6-10.

CAPSTAN NAVY CUT MILD - 50 cig.
W.D. & H.O. Wills, Bristol, UK, ca. 1935. $6-10.

CARAVAN - 10 cig.
National Tob. Co., India,
ca. 1950. $6-10.

CARIBE - 20 cig.
Cubatabaco, Cuba, ca. 1970. $1-5.

Captain Grant - 20 cig.
John Wood & Sons, Ltd., Holland,
ca. 1960. $1-5.

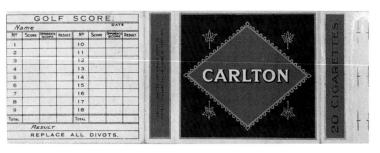

CARLTON - 20 cig.
Imperial Tob.Co., UK,
ca. 1930. $11-20.

CARLYLE VIRGINIA - 50 cig.
Martins Ltd. of Piccadilly,
UK, ca. 1930. $6-10.

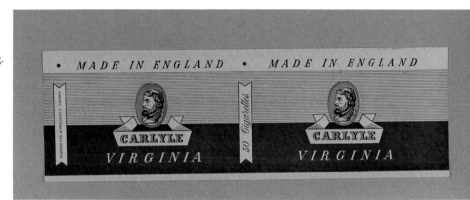

CARRERAS - 20 cig.
Carreras Ltd., London, UK, ca. 1980. $1-5.

Cavalcade - 10 cig.
Louis Gerard Ltd., UK,
ca. 1955. $1-5.

CARSON CITY - 20 cig.
Weeke & Kjaer A/S Copenhagen,
Denmark,
ca. 1950. $1-5.

CAVALIER - 20 cig.
R.J. Reynolds, Winston-Salem, NC,
USA, ca. 1955. $1-5.

CAVALIER - 100 cig.
R.J. Reynolds, Winston-Salem, USA, ca. 1950. Tin, $41-80.

CHAIRMAN JUNIOR - 10 cig.
R.J. Lea Ltd., Manchester, UK,
ca. 1955. $1-5.

CHAMPAGNE CANARD-DUCHENE - 3 cig.
Seita, France,
ca. 1970. $6-10.

CAVANDERS - 10 cig.
Made in India,
ca. 1960. $6-10.

CHAMPION - 3 cig.
United Tob. Factory,
Switzerland, ca. 1960. $1-5.

CHAMPION - 20 cig.
United Tobacco Factories,
Switzerland, ca. 1965. $1-5.

CHANCELLOR
Goodwin & Co., New York, N
USA, ca. 1890. $21-40.

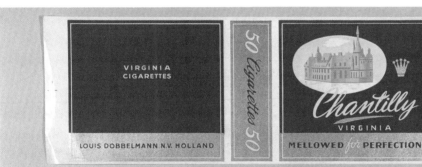

CHANTILLY - 50 cig.
Louis Dobbelmann NV,
Holland, ca. 1940. $6-10.

CHARLESTON - 20 cig.
Made in Denmark, ca. 1955. $1-5.

CHESTERFIELD - 50 cig.
L & M, Fact. No. 25, VA, USA,
ca. 1940. Tin, $21-40.

CHARLEMAGNE - 20 cig.
Tabacs Reig, Andorra,
ca. 1970. $1-5.

CHELSEA - 20 cig.
Larus Bros Richmond, VA, USA,
ca. 1943. $21-40.

CHERRY - 20 cig.
Made in Japan,
ca. 1972. $1-5.

CHERRY - 20 cig.
Made in Japan,
ca. 1972. $1-5.

CHERRY - 20 cig.
Made in Japan,
ca. 1973. $1-5.

CHERRY - 20 cig.
Made in Japan,
ca. 1978. $1-5.

CHERRY - 20 cig.
Made in Japan,
ca. 1972. $1-5.

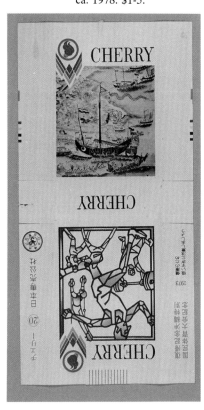

CHESS - 20 cig.
Hignett Bros & Co., London,
UK, ca. 1925. $6-10.

CHURCHMAN'S No. 1 - 50 cig.
W.A. & A.C. Churchman, Ipswich, UK,
ca. 1935. $6-10.

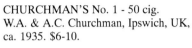

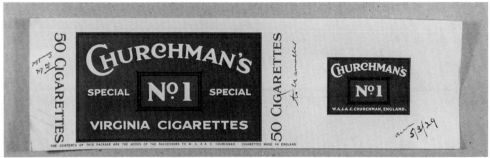

CHESTERFIELD - 9 cig.
L & M, USA,
ca. 1920. $21-40.

CHURCHMAN'S No. 1 - 50 cig.
W.A. & A.C. Churchman, Ipswich
UK, ca. 1930. $6-10.

CHESTERFIELD - 5 cig.
Liggett & Myers Tob. Co.,
USA - ca. 1940. $6-10.

CHESTERFIELD - 20 cig.
Liggett & Myers, California,
USA, ca. 1935. $6-10.

CHESTERFIELD -
20 cig.
Liggett & Myers
Tob. Co., Durham,
NC,
USA, ca. 1960. $1-
5.

CHIEF WHIP - 50 cig.
Ardath Tob. Co., London,
UK, ca. 1935. $6-10.

CHING & CO'S SILK CUT - 50 cig.
Ching & Co., Jersey, UK,
ca. 1930. $6-10.

CHEVRON - 20 cig.
BAT Indonesia,
ca. 1965. $1-5.

CIERVO - 20 cig.
Empresa Cubana del tabaco, Cuba, ca. 1970. $1-5.

CHESSMAN - 10 cig.
Svenska Tobacs Monopolet,
Sweden, ca. 1960. $1-5.

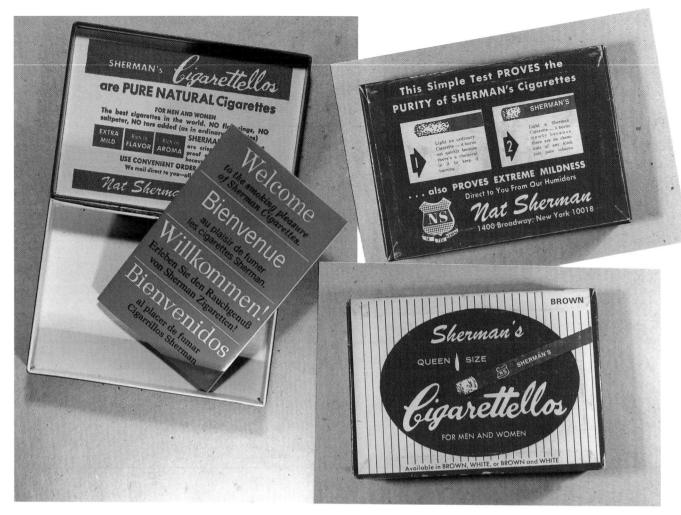

CIGARETTELLOS - 20 cig.
Nat Sherman, New York, NY,
USA, ca. 1975. $6-10.

CIGARETTES - 100 cig.
Regie des Tabacs de l'Empire Ottoman,
Turkey, ca. 1910. Tin, $11-20.

CIGARETTES DE TROUPE - 20 cig.
Regie Française de Tabacs,
France, ca. 1943. $6-10.

CIGARETTES DE LOUISVILLE - 50 cig.
W.D. & H.O. Wills, Bristol, UK, ca. 1955. $6-10.

CIGARETTES TURQUES - 100 cig.
Regie des tabacs de l'Empire, Ottoman,
Turkey, ca. 1910. Tin, $21-40.

12 O' CLOCK - 10 cig.
Silk Leaf Tob. Co., London, UK,
ca. 1950. $6-10.

COLONY - 20 cig.
The American Tob. Co.,
USA, ca. 1970. $6-10.

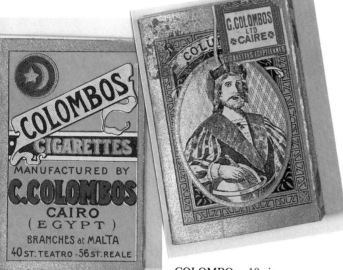

COLOMBOs - 10 cig.
C. Colombo, Malta,
ca. 1920. $6-10.

CLEOPATRA - 20 cig.
Made in Egypt,
ca. 1975. $1-5.

CLIPPER - 50 cig.
Player, UK, ca. 1940. $6-10.

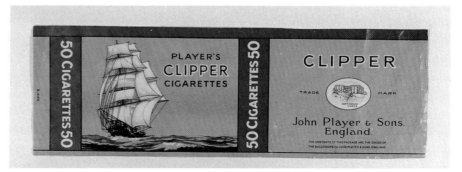

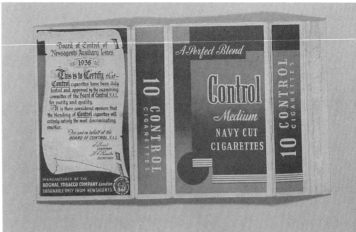

CONTROL - 10 cig.
Bognal Tob. Co., London,
UK, ca. 1935. $6-10.

CORT - 20 cig.
Riggio Tob. Corp., NY, USA,
ca. 1948. $11-20.

COCKTAIL - 20 cig.
United Cig. Fact., Holland, ca. 1950. $1-5.

COMMANDER - 50 cig.
Westminster Tob. Co., London, UK,
ca. 1935. $11-20.

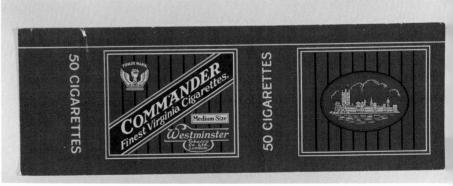

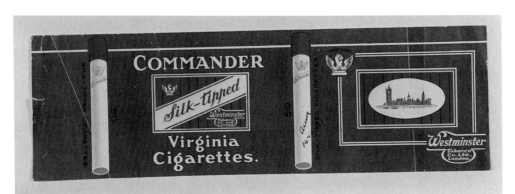

COMMANDER SILK TIPPED - 50
Westminster Tob. Co. Ltd., London,
UK, ca. 1930. $6-10.

CONSULATE - 50 cig.
Rothmans of Pall Mall,
UK, ca. 1950. $1-5.

COOLTIPT - 50 cig.
Abdulla & Co Ltd., London
UK, ca. 1940. $6-10.

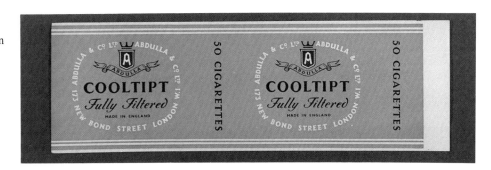

COLLEGE CIGARETTE
Bacon Bros, Cambridge, Bacon, UK,
ca. 1910. $6-10.

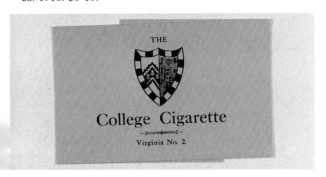

COLOMBO'S - 20 cig.
C. Colombo's Ltd.,
Malta, ca. 1925. $6-10.

CONGO - 20 cig.
Regie Française des tabacs, France,
ca. 1930. $6-10.

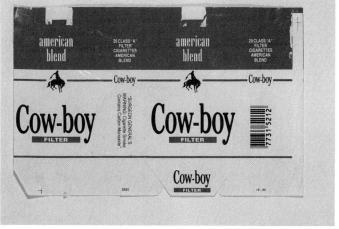

COW-BOY - 20 cig.
Made in USA,
ca. 1980. $1-5.

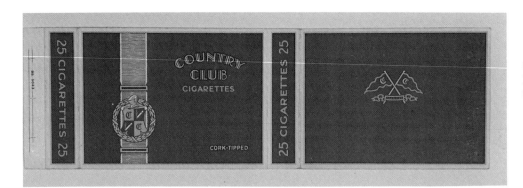

COUNTRY CLUB - 25 cig.
B.A.T., UK,
ca. 1960. $1-5.

COUNTRY LIFE - 50 cig.
J. Player, Nottingham, UK,
ca. 1935. $6-10.

CRAVEN "A" - 50 cig.
Carreras Ltd, London
UK - 1950 ca. - $ 6 - 10 - Tin

CORONITAS - 20 cig.
Hungarian Monopol, Hungary,
ca. 1940. $11-20

COUNTRY LIFE MAGNUM - 50 cig.
Player, UK, ca. 1925. $6-10.

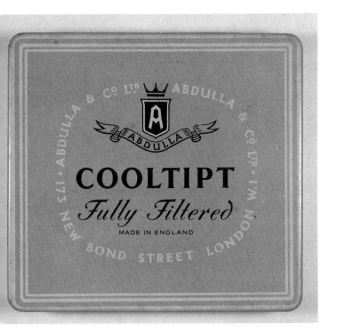

CRAVEN PLAIN - 50 cig.
Fact. no. 6, Canada
ca. 1955. $21-40.

COOLTIPT - 20 cig.
Abdulla & Co Ltd., London, UK, ca. 1950. Tin, $6-10.

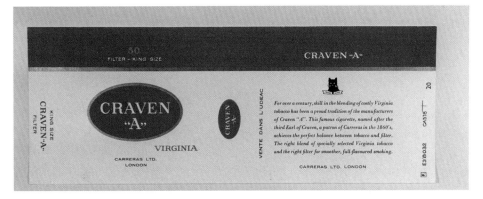

CRAVEN "A" - 50 cig.
Carreras Ltd., London,
UK, ca. 1950. Tin, $6-10.

CROWN BIRD - 10 cig.
E. Robinson & Sons Ltd.,
Indonesia, ca. 1950. $1-5.

CROCIERA AEREA XI - 10 cig.
Monopoli di Stato Italia, Italy,
ca. 1933. $80-200.

CROWN BIRD - 50 cig.
W.D. & H.O. Wills, Bristol, UK,
ca. 1930. $11-20.

CUMBERLAND - 20 cig.
Cert. a 92 Verde, Avellaneda, Argentina, ca. 1960. $1-5.

CURZON - 20 cig.
U.L. MacDonald, Canada, Holland, ca. 1960. $1-5.

CURZON - 50 cig.
Curzon Tob. Co. Ltd., London,
UK, ca. 1935. $6-10.

CROMWELL - 50 cig.
Bacon Bros, Cambridge, UK,
ca. 1920. $6-10.

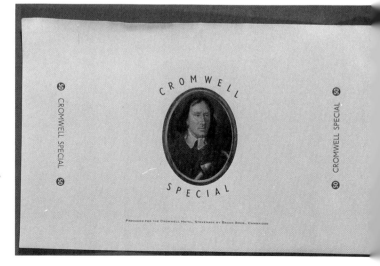

DAILY MAIL - 25 cig.
Consolidated Tob. Co., Montreal,
Canada, ca. 1960. $6-10.

DAVIS CUP - 20 cig.
Made in Denmark,
ca. 1955. $1-5.

DAMES - 50 cig.
Dohany Jovedek, Hungary,
ca. 1930. $11-20.

DAKOTA - 20 cig.
Made in Holland,
ca. 1945. $6-10.

DARU - 20 cig.
Magyar Dohanyigyar, Hungary,
ca. 1970. $1-5.

DAVROS - 50 cig.
D. Missirian Brussels, Belgium, ca. 1930. Tin, $21-40.

DE RESZKE MINORS - 30 cig.
G. Phillips, Melbourne,
Australia, ca. 1930. Tin, $11-20.

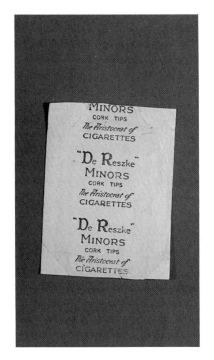

DAVROS - 20 cig.
D. Missirian, Brussels, Belgium, ca. 1932. $6-10.

DE RESZKE MINORS - 10 cig.
J. Millhof & Co., London, UK,
ca. 1943. $6-10.

DIAMOND - 10 cig.
Made in Pakistan,
ca. 1970. $1-5.

DE RESZKE - 50 cig.
J. Millhof & Co., London, UK, ca. 1930. Tin, $11-20.

DE RESZKE FILTER TIPPED - 10 cig.
J. Millhof & Co, Piccadilly, UK, ca. 1930. $6-10.

DE RESZKE BLUE LABEL - 20 cig.
J. Millhof & Co., London, UK, ca. 1935. $11-20.

DESTI - 25 cig.
Tartu Tob., Tallinn,
Estonia, ca. 1935. $11-20.

DEFINITIVOS - 10 cig.
A. Tabaqueira, Lisbon,
Portugal, ca. 1970. $1-5.

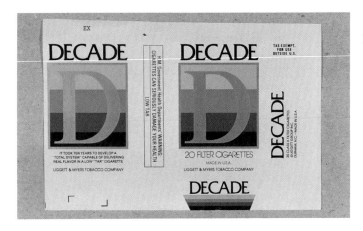

DECADE - 20 cig.
Liggett & Myers, USA, UK,
ca. 1975. $1-5.

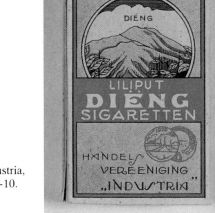

DIENG - 10 cig.
Handels Vereeniging, Industria,
South Africa, ca. 1925. $6-10.

DIANA - 25 cig.
Jacobs et Teurling, Brussels,
Belgium, ca. 1930. $6-10.

DOLCE VITA - 20 cig.
Societé Job, Geneva,
Switzerland, ca. 1965. $1-5.

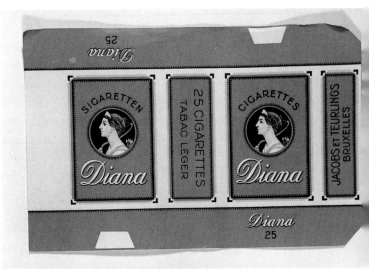

DIANA - 20 cig.
Tabacalera SA, Spain
ca. 1950. $6-10.

DIMITRINO - 20 cig.
Dimitrino & Co., Cairo, Egypt, ca. 1915. $41-80.

DIMITRINO - 20 cig.
Dimitrino & Co.
Cairo - Egypt
ca. 1920. Tin, $21-40.

DICE - 50 cig.
BAT, London
UK, ca. 1930. $6-10.

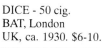

DIVINA - 20 cig.
Sauberli Fr., Switzerland,
ca. 1905. Tin, $21-40.

DOMINO - 4 cig.
Lambert & Butler, UK,
ca. 1935. $11-20.

DOBBELMANN'S DELIGHT - 20 cig.
Louis Dobbelmann NV,
Holland, ca. 1960. $1-5.

DOMINO - 20 cig.
Larus Bros, Richmond, VA, USA,
ca. 1960. $11-20.

DON CAMILLO - 20 cig.
Job, Geneva,
Switzerland, ca. 1960. $6-10.

DUNHILL - 3 cig.
Alfred Dunhill Ltd., London,
UK, ca. 1970. $1-5.

DUNHILL MAJORS - 20 cig.
Dunhill, VA, USA
ca. 1950. $6-10.

DOUBLE ACE - 10 cig.
Ardath Tob. Co., London, UK,
ca. 1960. $1-5.

DOUBLE ACE - 50 cig.
Ardath Tob. Co., London,
UK, ca. 1935. $6-10.

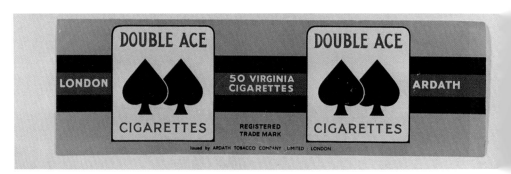

DRUMHEAD - 50 cig.
J. Player, Nottingham, UK, ca. 1935. $6-10.

DUNA - 20 cig.
Made in Hungary,
ca. 1980. $1-5.

DURHAM
Blackwell & Co., Durham, NC, USA, ca. 1890. $21-40.

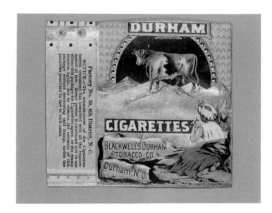

DURHAM
Blackwell's Durham Tob. Co., Durham, NC,
USA, ca. 1890. $21-40.

EDEN - 20 cig.
Winchester Tob. Co., Holland,
ca. 1960. $1-5.

EGIPSKIE - 20 cig.
Polski Monopol, Poland, ca. 1950. Tin, $6-10.

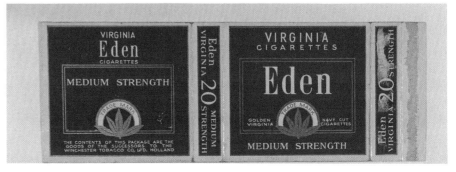

EAST COAST - 10 cig.
Made in Denmark, ca. 1950. $1-5.

EGYPTIAN PRETTIEST - 10 cig.
Schinasi Bros
USA, ca. 1925. $21-40.

EGYPTIAN BLEND No. 2 - 20 cig.
B. Muratti
& Sons Co., London,
UK, ca. 1925. $11-20.

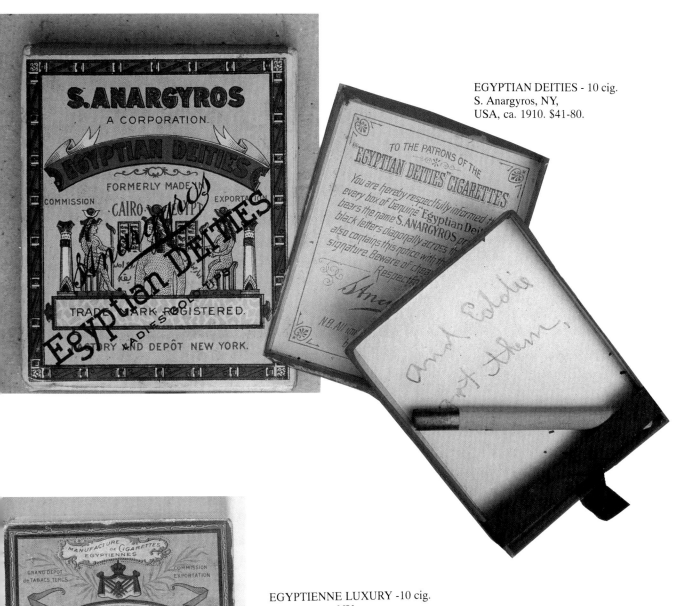

EGYPTIAN DEITIES - 10 cig.
S. Anargyros, NY,
USA, ca. 1910. $41-80.

EGYPTIENNE LUXURY -10 cig.
S. Anargyros, NY,
USA, ca. 1909. $41-80.

EGYPTO - 20 cig.
Trapani & Cia, Sao Paulo,
Brazil, ca. 1885. $6-10.

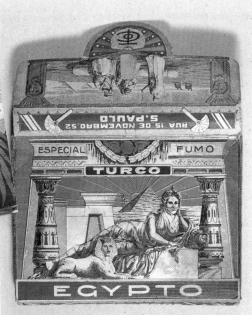

EIA EIA ALALÁ
Sabrati, Sao Paulo, Brazil,
ca. 1938. $11-20.

EJA - 10 cig.
Monopolio dei Tabacchi, Rome,
Italy, ca. 1930. $21-40.

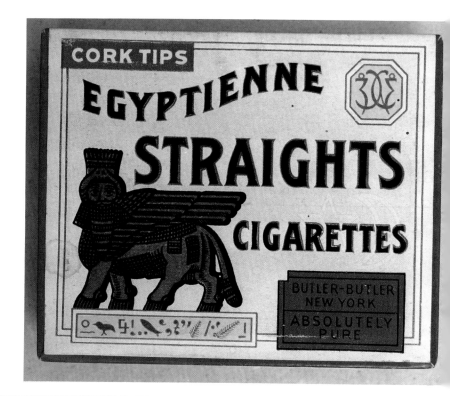

EIFFEL - 12 cig.
Made in Holland,
ca. 1950. $6-10.

EGYPTIENNE STRAIGHTS - 20 cig.
Butler, NY, USA, ca. 1920. $21-40.

ELEPHANT - 50 cig.
Thomas Bear & Sons, London, UK,
ca. 1930. $6-10.

ELEPHANT - 50 cig.
Thomas Bear & Sons
London, UK,
ca. 1935. $6-10.

EL AL - 20 cig.
Dubek Ltd., Tel Aviv,
Israel, ca. 1970. $1-5.

EL PASO - 25 cig.
Ed. Laurens Continental
Holland, ca. 1965. $1-5.

ELEPHANT - 10 cig.
Thomas Bear & Sons, London,
ca. 1920. $6-10.

ELSA KRUGER - 10 cig.
G.A. Jasmatzi, Dresden, Germany,
ca. 1900. $21-40.

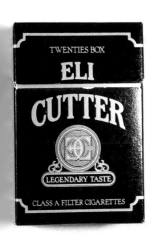

EMBASSY - 50 cig.
W.D. & H.O. Wills, Bristol,
UK, ca. 1930. $6-10.

ELI CUTTER - 20 cig.
B. & W., Louisville, KY, USA,
ca. 1970. $6-10.

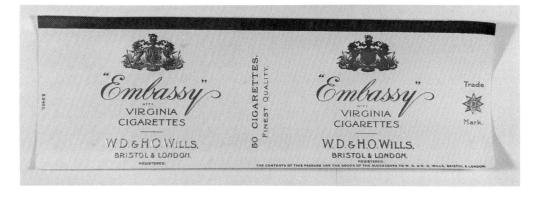

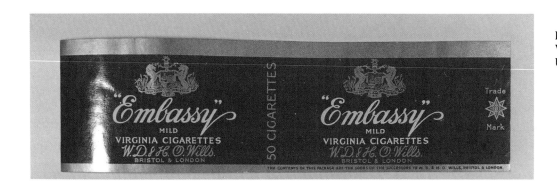

EMBASSY MILD - 50 cig.
W.D. & H.O. Wills, Bristol,
UK, ca. 1935. $6-10.

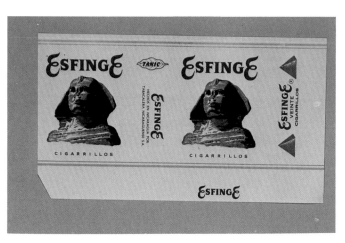

ESFINGE - 20 cig.
Tabacalera Nicaraguense SA,
Nicaragua, ca. 1975. $1-5.

ENEO FIUME - 10 cig.
Monopoli di Stato, Italy,
ca. 1930. $21-40.

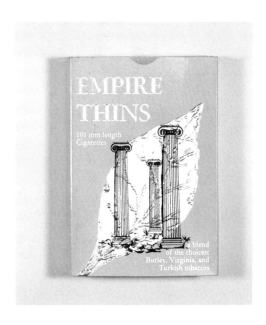

EMPIRE THINS - 20 cig.
Briki Tob. Co., Miami, FL,
USA, ca. 1975. $6-10.

ENGLISH OVALS - 20 cig.
P. Morris Inc, Richmond, VA,
USA, ca. 1950. $11-20.

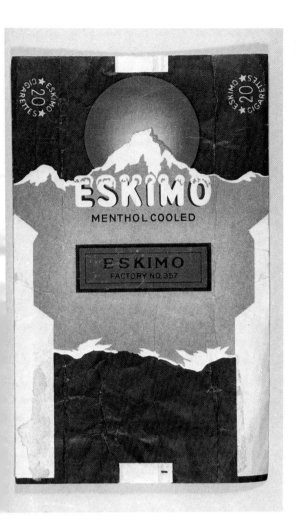

ESKIMO - 20 cig.
Factory no. 357,
Switzerland, ca. 1950. $1-5.

EXCEPCIONALES 43-20 cig.
Piccardo y C.ia, Uspallata, Argentina, ca. 1970. $1-5.

ESTONIA- 10 cig.
Leek, Tallinn, USSR,
ca. 1948. $11-20.

EUROPA - 3 cig.
Regie Monegasque
des Tabacs,
Monaco, ca. 1970. $1-5.

F.A.O. - 20 cig.
Egri Dohanigyar, Eger,
Hungary, ca. 1990. $1-5.

FAROS - 15 cig.
La Tabacalera Mexicana Sa,
Mexico, ca. 1960. $1-5.

FEAST DAY - 20 cig.
Le Berger, Holland,
ca. 1955. $1-5.

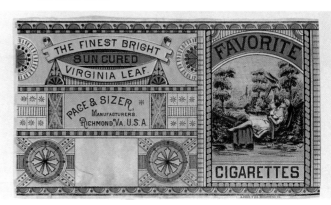

FAVORITE
Pace & Sizer, Richmond, VA,
USA, ca. 1890. $21-40.

FIFTEENS - 50 cig.
Amalgamated Tob. Corp., Luton, UK,
ca. 1935. $6-10.

FESTIVAL - 20 cig.
Yava, Moscow, USSR,
ca. 1950. $6-10.

FEMINA - 20 cig.
Made in Bulgaria,
ca. 1960. $1-5.

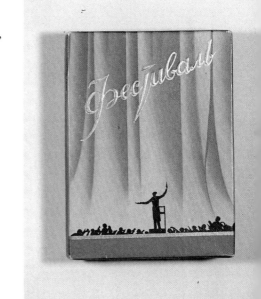

FIFTH AVENUE - 20 cig.
Abdulla & Co Ltd., London,
UK, ca. 1950. $1-5.

FIFTY FIFTY - 20 cig.
Goodwin & Co., New York, NY,
USA, ca. 1940. $6-10.

FIVE STARS - 20 cig.
Stephano Bros, Philadelphia,
USA, ca. 1935. $21-40.

FIGHTER - 10 cig.
Louis Gerard, UK,
ca. 1940. $11-20.

FILTERTIPS - 10 cig.
Amalgamated Tob. Corp., Luton,
UK, ca. 1955. $1-5.

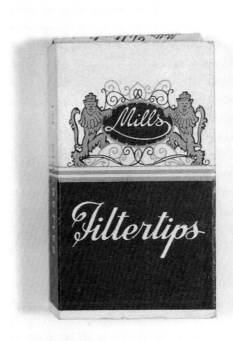

FIORAVANTI - 50 cig.
Fioravanti Cig. co., Port Said, Egypt, ca. 1910 ca Tin, $21-40.

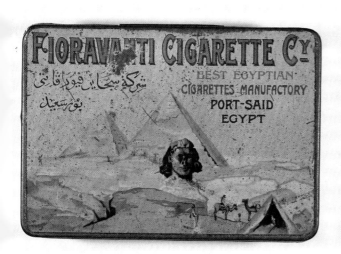

FONTANARES No. 12 - 20 cig.
Cert. A 68 Verde, Buenos Aires,
Argentina, ca. 1955. $1-5.

FOLK'S OWN - 10 cig.
Souvenir Tob. Co. Ltd.,
Pakistan, ca. 1965. $1-5.

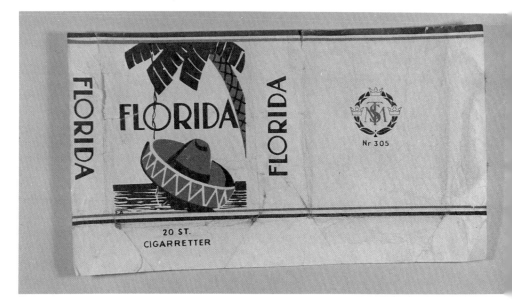

FLIRT - 20 cig.
Austria Tabakwerke, Austria,
ca. 1980. $1-5.

FLORIDA - 20 cig.
Svenska Tobaks Monopolet,
Sweden, ca. 1950. $1-5.

FOUR ACES - 10 cig.
Wills, Bristol, UK, ca. 1940. $6-10.

FOUR ACES - 50 cig.
W.D. & H.O. Wills, Bristol
UK, ca. 1930. $6-10.

FOUR ACES CORK TIPPED - 50 cig.
W.D. & H.O. Wills, Bristol, UK, ca. 1930. $6-10.

FOUR ACES MAGNUMS - 50 cig.
W.D. & H.O. Wills, Bristol,
UK, ca. 1922. $6-10.

FOUR ACES CORK TIPPED - 50 cig.
W.D. & H.O. Wills, Bristol, UK,
ca. 1930. $6-10.

FUJI - 10 cig.
Made in Japan, ca. 1965. $1-5.

FREGATE - 3 cig.
Manufacture des Tabacs, Geneva,
Switzerland ca. 1970. $1-5.

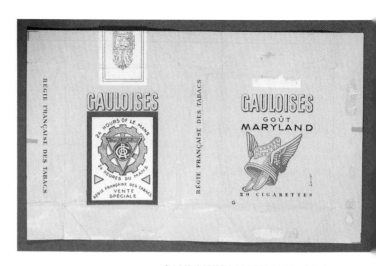

GAULOISES MARYLAND - 20 cig.
Regie Française des Tabacs,
France, ca. 1970. $1-5.

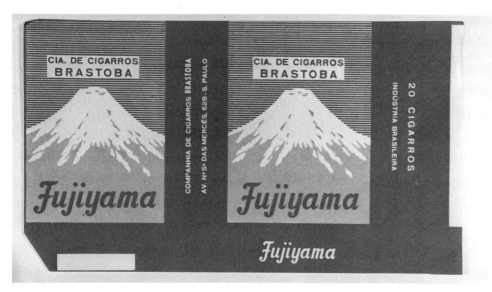

FUJIYAMA - 20 cig.
Brastoba, Sao Paulo,
Brazil, ca. 1960. $1-5.

GAULOISES BLUE WAY - 20 cig.
Seita, France,
ca. 1980. $1-5.

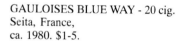

GALLAHER'S NAVY CUT - 50 cig.
Gallaher Ltd., London, UK,
ca. 1930. $6-10.

GAULOISES DISQUE BLEU - 20 cig.
Regie Française des tabacs, France, ca. 1975. $1-5.

GIB - 5 cig.
Carreras Ltd., London, UK,
ca. 1920. $41-80.

GELBE SORTE - 10 cig.
Reemtsma Gmbh, Hamburg,
Germany, ca. 1930. $6-10.

GIDON - 10 cig.
Reemtsma, Hamburg,
Germany, ca. 1910. $11-20.

GENERAL MOTORS - 10 cig.
Monopoli di Stato, Italy,
ca. 1960. $11-20.

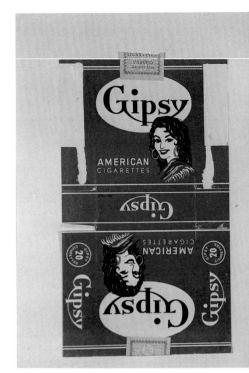

GIPSY - 20 cig.
Yabuco, Amsterdam,
Holland, ca. 1970. $1-5.

GIDON - 50 cig.
Reemtsma Hamburg, Germany,
ca. 1920. $11-20.

GIBSON GIRL - 10 cig.
Manoli Cig., Hamburg, Germany,
ca. 1920. $11-20.

GINSENG - 20 cig.
Changchun Cig. Fact., China,
ca. 1975. $1-5.

GITANES - 5 cig.
Seita, France,
ca. 1970. $1-5.

GLADIATOR - 10 cig.
Redford & Co., London
UK, ca. 1925. $6-10.

GITANES - 20 cig.
Seita, France, ca. 1938. $11-20.

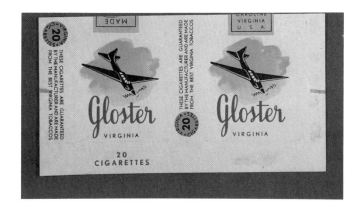

GLOSTER - 20 cig.
Made in Holland,
ca. 1950. $1-5.

GOLD FLAKE - 10 cig.
W.D. & H.O. Wills, Bristol, UK,
ca. 1935. $6-10.

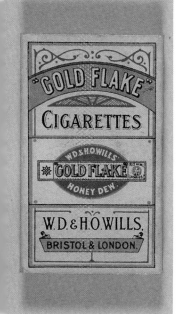

GLACIER - 50 cig.
W.D. & H.O. Wills, Bristol, UK,
ca. 1930. $11-20.

GO TO HELL! - 20 cig.
GTH, Inc. NJ, USA,
ca. 1975. $6-10.

GOLD CITY - 20 cig.
Thailand Tobacco Monopoly, Thailand, ca. 1980. $1-5.

GOLD CUP - 20 cig.
Roberts, Switzerland, ca. 1948. $1-5.

GOLD FLAKE - 50 cig.
Wills, Bristol, UK, ca. 1925. Tin, $11-20.

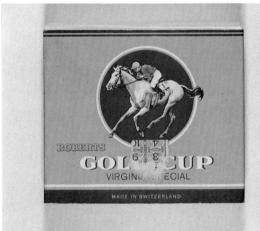

GOLD FLAKE - 50 cig.
W.D. & H.O. Wills, Bristol,
UK, ca. 1935. Tin, $11-20.

GOLD FLAKE - 50 cig.
W.D. & H.O. Wills, Bristol, UK, ca. 1925. $6-10

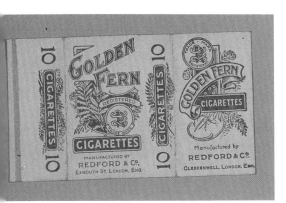

GOLDEN FERN - 10 cig.
Redford & Co., London, UK,
ca. 1930. $11-20.

GRAFIN MARIZA - 50 cig.
Jasmatzi Gmbh, Germany, ca. 1910. $21-40.

GOLDEN JACK - 20 cig.
Warwichs Factory Cigarettes,
Denmark, ca. 1948. $6-10.

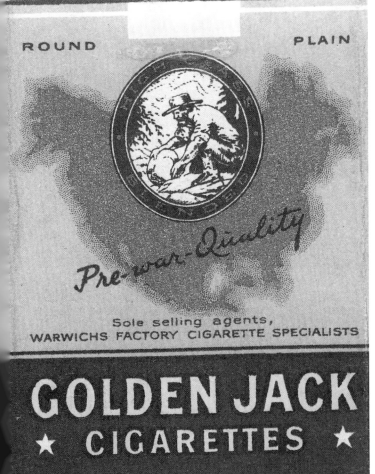

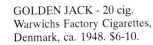

GPO - 10 cig.
John Sinclair, UK, ca. 1950. $1-5

GOLDEN SPECIALS - 25 cig.
BAT, UK, ca. 1930. $6-10.

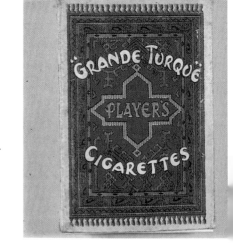

GRANDE TURQUE - 10 cig.
J. Player, Nottingham, UK,
ca. 1935. $6-10.

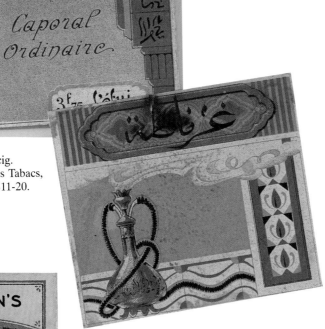

GRENADES - 20 cig.
Regie Française des Tabacs,
France, ca. 1930. $11-20.

GRAND MASTER 5 UP - 10 cig.
Asia Tob. Co. Ltd., Singapore,
ca. 1935. $1-5.

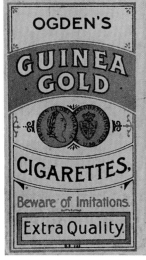

GUINEA GOLD SPECIALS - 50 cig.
Ogden of Liverpool
UK, ca. 1935. $6-10.

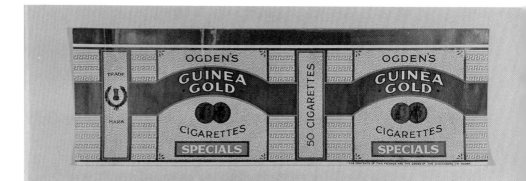

GUINEA GOLD - 10 cig.
Ogden of Liverpool, UK,
ca. 1930. $11-20.

GUINEA GOLD - 50 cig.
Ogden of Liverpool
UK, ca. 1930. Tin, $41-80.

GUINEA GOLD - 50 cig.
Ogden of Liverpool, UK,
ca. 1935. $6-10.

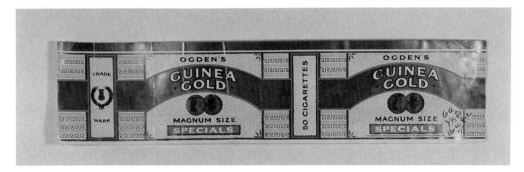

HALPAUS RARITAT - 25 cig.
Eckstein-Halpaus, Dresden,
Germany, ca. 1935. $6-10.

HARE RAMA - 25 cig.
Wikram Int., Bombay,
India, ca. 1975. $1-5.

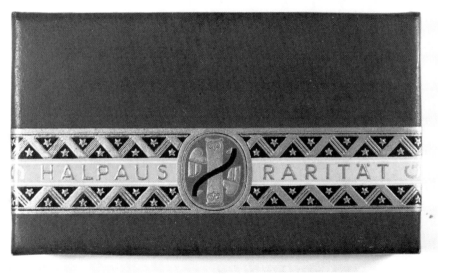

HAPPY HIT - 20 cig.
The American Tob. Co., NY, USA,
ca. 1940. $11-20.

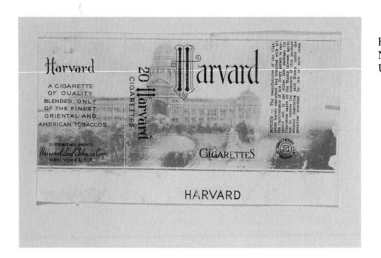

HARVARD - 20 cig.
National Leaf Tob. Corp., NY,
USA, ca. 1940. $11-20.

HASSAN - 20 cig.
American Tob. Co., Fact. No. 30, N
USA, ca. 1930. $21-40.

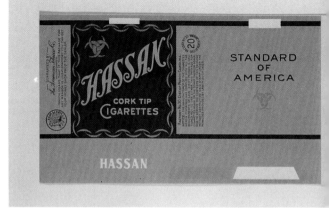

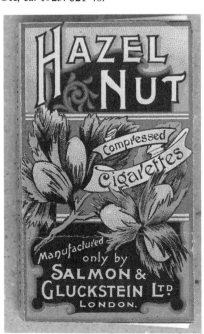

HASSAN - 20 cig.
The Anglo-American Cig. Co.,
Holland, ca. 1940. $6-10.

HAVANA BLACKS - 20 cig.
U.L. Trinidad y Hermano, Cuba,
ca. 1985. $1-5.

HAZEL NUT - 10 cig.
Salmon & Gluckstein, London,
UK, ca. 1925. $21-40.

HELLAS SPECIAL - 20 cig.
Papastratos, Athens, Greece, ca. 1975. $1-5.

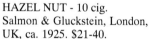

HIGH LIFE - 10 cig.
Made in Denmark,
ca. 1950. $6-10.

HYDE PARK - 20 cig.
Made in Holland,
ca. 1950. $1-5.

HIGH CLASS - 20 cig.
Teofani & Co., London, UK,
ca. 1940-ca. $11-20.

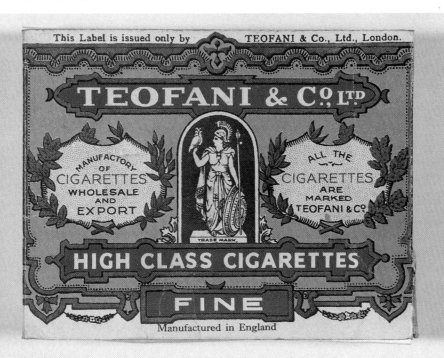

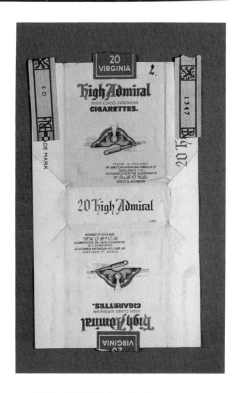

HIGH ADMIRAL - 20 cig.
BAT, Holland,
ca. 1950. $1-5.

HERTENSTRIKKER - 10 cig.
The Eastern Virg. Cig. Co., Holland
ca. 1935. $6-10.

HONG KONG - 10 cig.
J. Hediger, Bienne,
Switzerland, ca. 1929. $11-20.

HOFLOBNITZ - 10 cig.
Delta, Dresden, Germany,
ca. 1910. $6-10.

HIGH GRADE - 10 cig.
Kimball Co., Rochester, NY,
USA, ca. 1883. $41-80.

HOME RUN - 20 cig.
Fact. No. 7, VA, USA, ca. 1935. $21-40.

HI-LITE - 20 cig.
Made in Japan,
ca. 1980. $1-5.

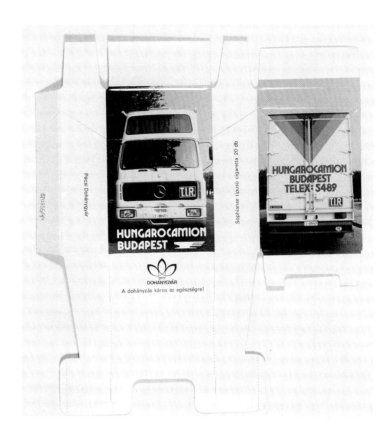

HUNGAROCAMION BUDAPEST - 20 cig.
Pecsi Dohanygiar,
Hungary, ca. 1990. $1-5.

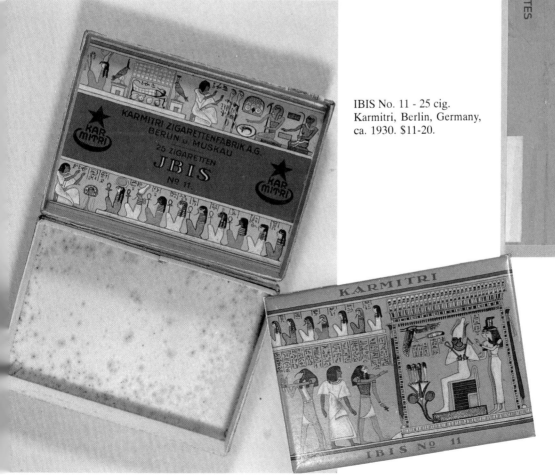

IBIS No. 11 - 25 cig.
Karmitri, Berlin, Germany,
ca. 1930. $11-20.

ICEBERG - 20 cig.
Made in Indonesia,
ca. 1960. $1-5.

IBIS - 20 cig.
Simon Arzt, Alexandria,
Egypt, ca. 1960. $6-10.

IMPERADOR - 20 cig.
C.ia Lopes Sa, S. Cruz do Sul,
Brazil, ca. 1955. $1-5.

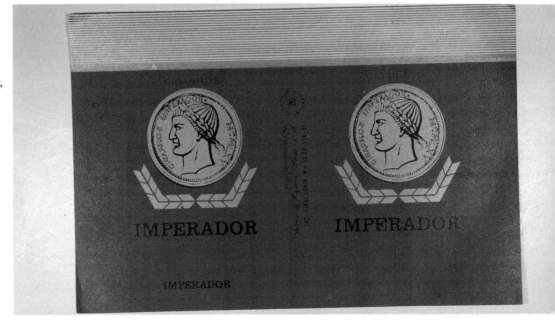

IMPERIAL PREFERENCE - 50 cig.
Abdulla & Co., London,
UK, ca. 1935. Tin, $6-10.

IMPALA - 20 cig.
C.ia Portuguesa de Tabacos,
Portugal, ca. 1965. $1-5.

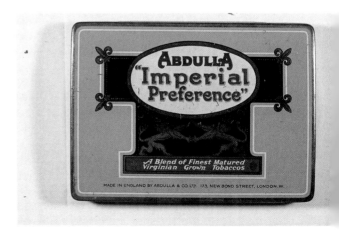

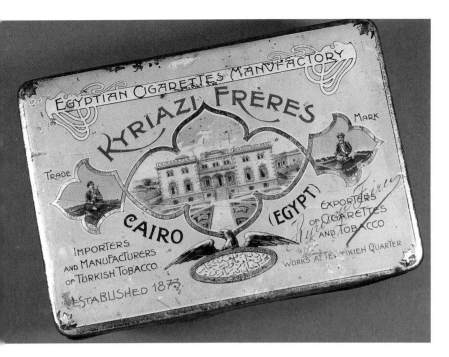

IMPERIAL PREFERENCE - 10 cig.
Abdulla & Co., London, UK,
ca. 1935. $6-10.

IMPERATORE - 100 cig.
Kyriazi Fr. Cairo, Egypt, ca. 1925. Tin, $41-80.

IMPERIAL SPECIALS - 50 cig.
Arcadian Tob. Co. Ltd., Calcutta, India, ca. 1930. $6-10.

IMPERIAL PREFERENCE - 10 cig.
Abdulla & Co Ltd., London, UK,
ca. 1950. $1-5.

IMPERIAL PREFERENCE - 50 cig.
Abdulla & Co Ltd., London, UK,
ca. 1940. $6-10.

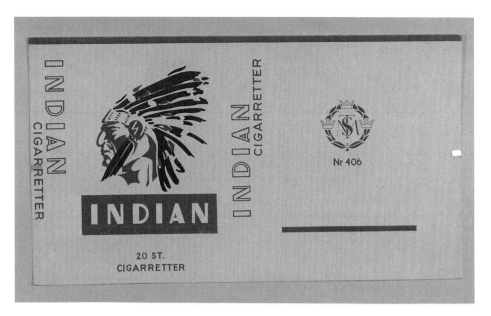

INDIAN - 20 cig.
Svenska Tobacs Monopolet,
Sweden, ca. 1950. $1-5.

ISLAND LONGS - 20 cig.
Briki Tob. Co.,
Miami, FL, USA
ca. 1965. $6-10.

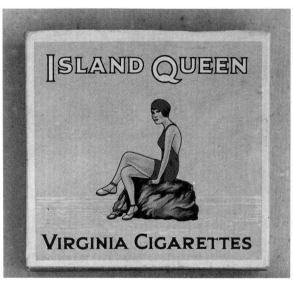

ISLAND QUEEN - 20 cig.
Murray & Sons, UK, ca. 1930. $21-40.

IRMA - 10 cig.
A.G. Cousis, Malta,
ca. 1910-ca. $6 -10.

IRONSIDES n_ 1-50 cig.
Finlay & Co. Ltd., London,
UK, ca. 1934. $6-10.

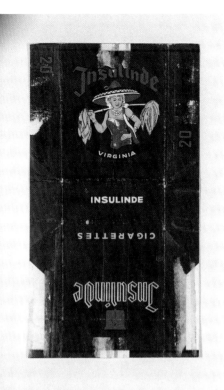

INSULINDE - 20 cig.
Made in Indonesia,
ca. 1960. $1-5.

JEZEBEL - 20 cig.
Georgopulo, New York, NY, USA,
ca. 1970. Rose perfumed, $6-10.

JEUX OLYMPIQUES D'HIVER - 10 cig.
Seita, France, ca. 1968. $6-10.

JUNO - 5 cig.
Josetti, Berlin, Germany
ca. 1925. $6-10.

JADRAN EXPORT - 20 cig.
Monopole d'etat du Royaume de Jugoslavie,
Yugoslavia, ca. 1930. $6-10

JIRAFA - 20 cig.
Tabacalera Sa, Spain,
ca. 1965. $1-5.

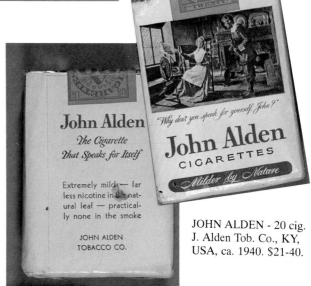

JOHN ALDEN - 20 cig.
J. Alden Tob. Co., KY,
USA, ca. 1940. $21-40.

JOHNNIE WALKER - 20 cig.
American Tob. Co., NC,
USA, ca. 1935. $21-40.

JUBILEAUM - 10 cig.
Monopoli di Stato, Italy,
ca. 1950. Holy Year, $21-40.

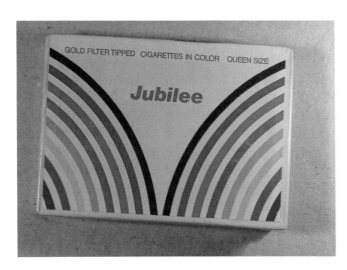

JUBILEE - 20 cig.
Nat Sherman, New York, NY, USA,
ca. 1970. $6-10.

KANARIS N0. 1 - 20 cig.
Kanaris Cigarettes, Holland
ca. 1960. $1-5.

K-2 - 10 cig.
Premier Tob. Ind. Ltd.,
Pakistan, ca. 1955. $6-10.

KEFIR - 10 cig.
Orient Cig. Co., Cairo, Egypt
ca. 1925. Tin, $21-40.

KEY - 10 cig.
Cope Bros, Liverpool, UK,
ca. 1930. $21-40.

KARAVAN - 25 cig.
La Ferme, Tallinn, Estonia
ca. 1935. $11-20.

KHEDIVE MOYEN -
20 cig.
Sullivan Powell,
Burlington Arcade, UK,
ca. 1975. $1-5.

KENSITAS - 50 cig.
J. Wix & Sons, London,
UK, ca. 1950. Tin, $11-20.

KHEDIVE - 25 cig.
Kosmos Gmbh, Dresden,
Germany, ca. 1925. Tin, $21-40.

KING STORK - 10 cig.
W.D. & H.O. Wills, Bristol, UK,
ca. 1950. $1-5.

KING SHIP - 20 cig.
Le Berger, Holland,
ca. 1950. $1-5.

KING'S GUARD - 10 cig.
Teofani & Co., London,
UK, ca. 1955. $6-10.

KORFU' ROT - 12 cig.
Made in Germany, ca. 1935. $11-20.

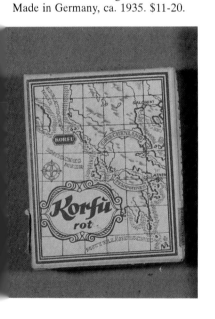

KINGS GATE - 50 cig.
Rothmans, London, UK, ca. 1960. Tin, $21-40.

KIRGIES - 20 cig.
J. Van Kerckof, Amsterdam,
Holland, ca. 1950. $1-5

KING'S PARADE - 20 cig.
Made in Holland,
ca. 1960. $1-5.

KNOTS - 25 cig.
Teofani & Co, UK,
ca. 1920. $11-20.

KOOA - 20 cig.
Made in Japan,
ca. 1930. $21-40.

KOOL - 20 cig.
B & W, Louisville, KY,
USA, ca. 1950. $6-10.

KOOL - 20 cig.
B & W, Fact. No. 30, KY, USA,
ca. 1943. War Bonds and Stamps, $21-40.

KYRIAZI FRERES - 100 cig.
Kyriazi Freres, Cairo, Egypt, ca. 1915. Tin, $21-40.

KYMAHOBKA - 20 cig.
Tytyyhob Kom., Kumanovo - Yugoslavie, ca. 1965. $1-5.

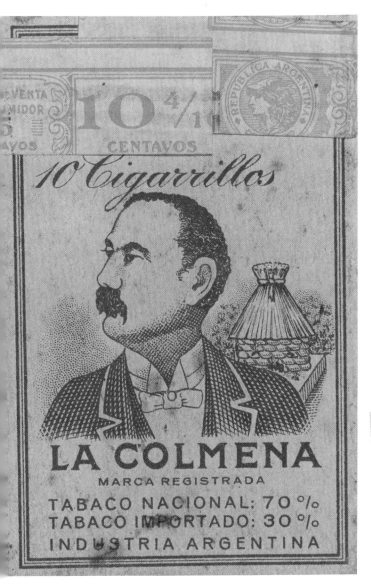

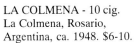

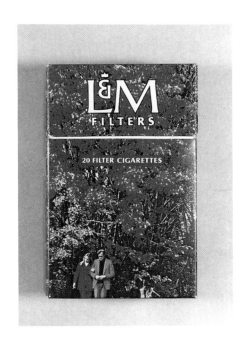

L & M FILTERS - 20 cig.
Liggett & Myers Inc., USA, ca. 1970. $1-5.

LA COLMENA - 10 cig.
La Colmena, Rosario,
Argentina, ca. 1948. $6-10.

L & M - 4 cig.
Liggett & Myers Tob. Co.
Durham, NC, USA, ca. 1968. $6-10.

LA CARMENCITA - 24 cig.
La Libertad Sa, Zamora, Mexico
ca. 1975. $1-5.

LA SERENA - 30 cig.
La Campana Fabrica de Tabacos Inc.,
Philippines, ca. 1960. $1-5.

LA FLOR DE NAPINTAS - 30 cig.
La Campana Fabrica de Tabacos Inc.,
Philippines, ca. 1965. $1-5.

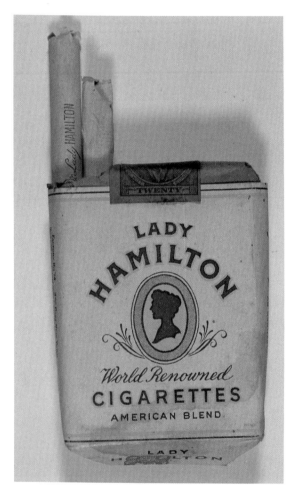

LADY HAMILTON - 20 cig.
J. & B. Soter Tob. Corp., NY,
USA, ca. 1935. $6-10.

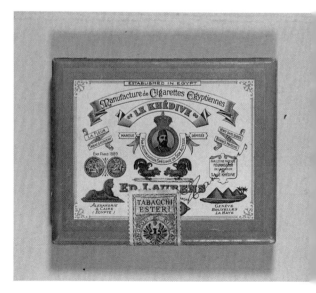

LE KHÈDIVE No. 15 - 20 cig.
Laurens, Cairo, Egypt
ca. 1937. Tin, $6-10.

LE KHEDIVE
Bros, Cambridge,
Bacon, UK, ca. 1910. $6-10

LAUREL - 20 cig.
N. Sarony, Piccadilly, London, UK, ca. 1930. $11-20.

LIBERTY - 20 cig.
American Tob. Co. A/S, Denmark
ca. 1955. $1-5.

LEVANTEBLUME - 10 cig.
Cig. Constantin, Dresden,
Germany, ca. 1916. $11-20.

LIBERTÉ - 20 cig.
Bat, UK, ca. 1950. $11-20.

LEGATION - 50 cig.
Arcadian Tob. Co. Ltd., UK,
ca. 1930. $6-10.

LIFE BOAT - 100 cig.
Salmon & Gluckstein, London, UK,
ca. 1910. Tin, $80-200.

LJETNE IGRE DUBROVNIK - 20 cig.
Tvornica Duhana Zadar, Yugoslavia, ca. 1965. $1-5.

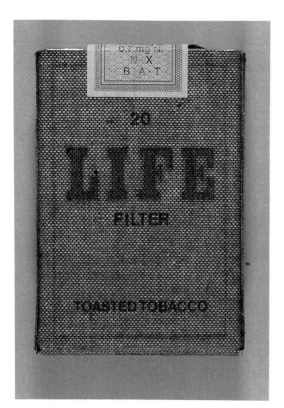

LIFE - 20 cig.
BAT Germany,
ca. 1980. $1-5.

LONDON IDOL - 50 cig.
R. & J. Hill Ltd., London,
UK, ca. 1930. $6-10.

LONDON IDOL - 10 cig.
R.J. Hill, London, UK,
ca. 1930. $11-20.

LORD SALISBURY - 20 cig.
American Tob. Co., Fact. No. 30, NC,
USA, ca. 1930. $6-10.

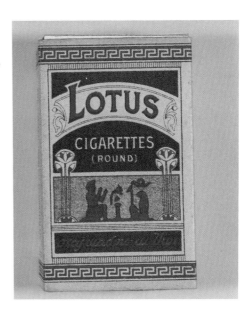

LOTUS - 10 cig.
The United Tob. Co., Ltd.,
South Africa, ca. 1930. $11-20.

LUCKY STRIKE - 20 cig.
The American Tob. Co., NC,
USA, ca. 1935. $21-40.

LUCKY STRIKE - 50 cig.
Bat, NY, USA, ca. 1935. Tin, $21-40.

LUCKY STRIKE
5 cig. - Made in USA,
USA, ca. 1970. $1-5.

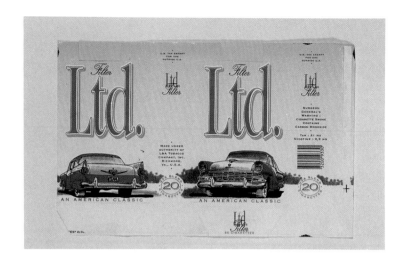

Ltd. - 20 cig.
L. & A. Tob. Co., Richmond, VA,
USA, ca. 1990. $1-5.

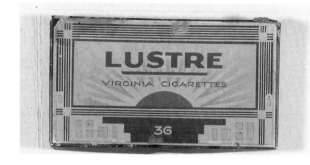

LUSTRE - 36 cig.
Made in UK,
ca. 1895. $21-40.

LUXOR - 20 cig.
Continental Cig. Co., Brussels, Belgium,
ca. 1920. Tin, $11-20.

LUCKY STRIKE - 10 cig.
B.A.T. Fact. No. 30, NC,
USA, ca. 1935. $11-20.

LUXUS - 25 cig.
Magyar Dohanyipar, Hungary
ca. 1968. $1-5.

LUCHADORES - 18 cig.
La Libertad Sa, Zamora, Mexico, ca. 1970. $1-5.

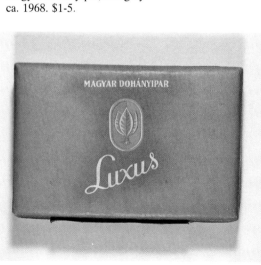

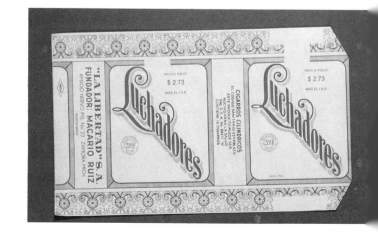

MAHARLIKA - 30 cig.
La Campana Fabrica de Tabacos Inc., Philippines, ca. 1965. $1-5.

MARVELS - 20 cig.
Stephano Bros, Successors,
USA, ca. 1960. $6-10.

MACDONALD'S GOLD STANDARD - 50 cig.
Imperial Tob. Co., Montreal,
Canada, ca. 1950. Tin, $11-20.

MARLBORO - 50 cig.
P. Morris Inc, Richmond
USA, ca. 1960. Tin, $11-20.

MARICH'S CIGARETTES - 50 cig.
Marich, Malta, ca. 1920. $6-10.

LUNA - 20 cig.
Magyar Dohanyipar,
Hungary, ca. 1970. $1-5.

MANON - 20 cig.
Compagnie La Ferme, Tallin,
Estonia, ca. 1935. $6-10.

MAEVA - 20 cig.
Seita, France, ca. 1980. $1-5.

MAJORET - 20 cig.
Made in Denmark,
ca. 1965. $1-5.

MAGKAIBIGAN - 30 cig.
La Campana Fabrica de Tabacos Inc.,
Philippines, ca. 1965. $1-5.

MARVELS - 20 cig.
Fact. No. 2032, Penna., USA, ca. 1960. $6-10.

MARLBORO - 4 cig.
Philip Morris, Inc, Richmond, VA.,
USA, ca. 1975. $1-5.

MAROCAINE - 20 cig.
SA Vautier Freres Cie, Yverdon,
Switzerland, ca. 1970. $1-5.

MARVEL - 8 cig.
Carlton Cig. Co. Ltd., Salisbury,
Rhodesia, ca. 1950. $6-10.

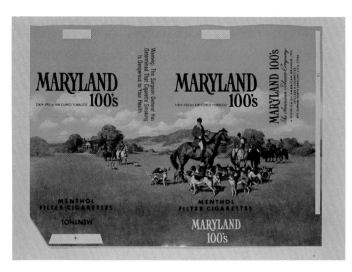

MARYLAND 100'S - 20 cig.
American Tob. Co., Durham, NC, USA, ca. 1975. $1-5.

MARY LONG - 20 cig.
BAT, Geneva, Switzerland, ca. 1955-65-75. $1-5.

MATAMIS - 20 cig.
La Campana Fabrica de Tabacos Inc.,
Philippines, ca. 1965. $1-5.

MASTERS - 20 cig.
Masters Tob. Co. Ltd., London,
UK, ca. 1955. $1-5.

MARYLAND AMERICAINES - 20 cig.
Thelos, Zurich,
Switzerland, ca. 1960. $1-5.

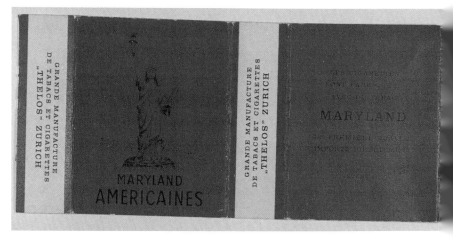

MATOSSIAN - 20 cig.
Matossian SA, Cairo. Egypt, ca. 1925. $11-20.

MASERATI - 10 cig.
Monopoli di Stato, Italy,
ca. 1960. $11-20.

MAXIM - 20 cig.
Pete Bros, Scandinavian Tob. Co., Denmark
ca. 1975. $1-5.

MATINÈE - 20 cig.
Lambert & Butler of Drury Lane,
UK, ca. 1960. $1-5.

MECCA - 20 cig.
The American Tob. Co., USA, ca. 1935. $21-40.

MECCA - 10 cig.
The American Tob. Co., USA
ca. 1920. $41-80.

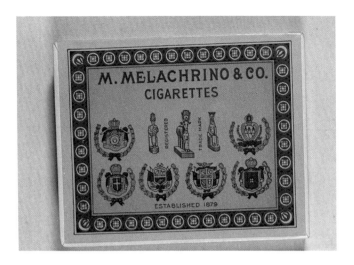

MELACHRINO - 20 cig.
American Tob. Co., USA,
ca. 1935. Tin, $21-40.

MELACHRINO No. 8 - 24 cig.
Melachrino & Co. NY, USA
ca. 1910. Tin, $41-80.

MELACHRINO No. 50 - 50 cig.
M. Melachrino & Co., London, UK,
ca. 1935. $11-20.

MELACHRINO No. 7 - 50 cig.
M. Melachrino & Co., London,
UK, ca. 1930. $6-10.

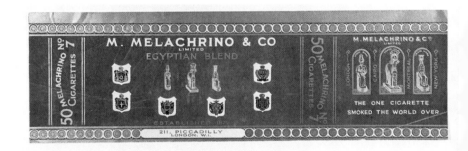

MELACHRINO No. 20 - 50 cig.
M. Melachrino & Co., London, UK, ca. 1930. $6-10.

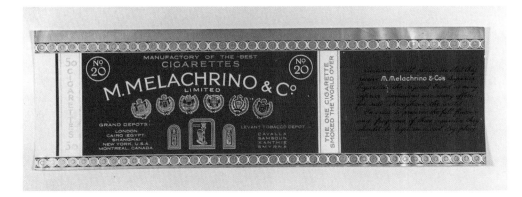

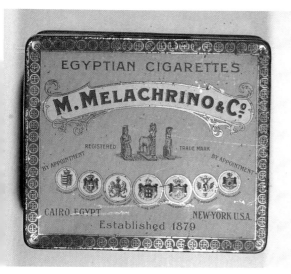

M. MELACHRINO - 50 cig.
M. Melachrino & Co., NY, USA, ca. 1920. Tin, $41-80.

MEMPHIS - 10 cig.
Factory & nation unknown, ca. 1920. $11-20.

MEMMOR (MEMENTO MORI) - 25 cig.
Made in Holland,
ca. 1980. $6-10.

MEMPHIS - 25 cig.
Osterreich Tabak Regie, Austria, ca. 1960. $6-10.

MES PASSIONS - 20 cig.
Garbaty Cig., Berlin,
Germany, ca. 1900. Tin, $11-20.

MERMAID - 20 cig.
The American Tob. Co.,
Durham, NC, USA,
ca. 1975. $1-5.

MEVA - 20 cig.
Made in Egypt,
ca. 1910. Tin, $41-80.

METROPOLE - 20 cig.
Made in Denmark,
ca. 1960. $1-5.

MILD SEVEN - 20 cig.
Japan Monopoly, Japan, ca. 1970. $1-5.

MICHIGAN - 10 cig.
Made in Sweden,
ca. 1960. $1-5.

MILLA - 20 cig.
Athanasiou & Co., Soleure,
Switzerland, ca. 1950. $1-5.

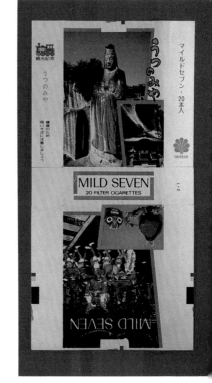

MILLA - 20 cig.
J. Athanasiou, Berne,
Switzerland,
ca. 1940. $6-10.

MILLS SPECIAL - 20 cig.
Amalgamated Tob. Co.,
Johannesburg, South Africa, ca. 1960. $1-5.

MILD SEVEN - 20 cig.
Made in Japan, ca. 1980. $1-5.

MILD SEVEN - 20 cig.
Made in Japan,
ca. 1981. $1-5.

MISS BLANCHE - 20 cig.
N.V. The Vittoria Egypt,
Rotterdam, Holland
ca. 1940. $1-5.

MISS BLANCHE - 20 cig.
Made in Holland,
ca. 1970. $1-5.

MISS BLANCHE EGYPTIAN - 10 cig.
The Vittoria Eg., Brussels, Belgium
ca. 1950. $6-10.

MISS BLANCHE - 25 cig.
BAT Holland,
ca. 1975. $1-5.

MISS BLANCHE GOLD LEAF - 10 cig.
The Vittoria Eg. Cig. Co., UK,
ca. 1940. $21-40.

MISS BLANCHE - 25 cig.
Made in Holland,
ca. 1965. $1-5.

MISTER X - 20 cig.
The Combined Tob. Co., Holland
ca. 1950. $1-5.

MONTECRISTO - 20 cig.
Cubatabaco, Cuba, ca. 1975. $1-5.

MISS BLANCHE VIRGINIA - 20 cig.
Made in Holland,
ca. 1955. $1-5.

MONTANA - 20 cig.
Cert. A 92 Verde, Avellaneda, Argentina, ca. 1950. $1-5.

MOHAWK - 10 cig.
B. Morris & Sons, London,
UK, ca. 1935. $11-20.

MOSCOWSKJE - 25 cig.
Dukat, Moscow, USSR
ca. 1955. $6-10.

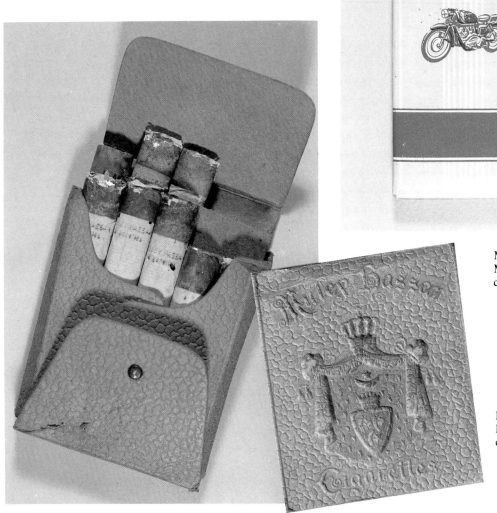

MOTO GUZZI - 10 cig.
Monopoli di Stato, Italy
ca. 1960. $11-20.

MULEY HASSAN - 10 cig.
Made in Turkey,
ca. 1890. $11-20.

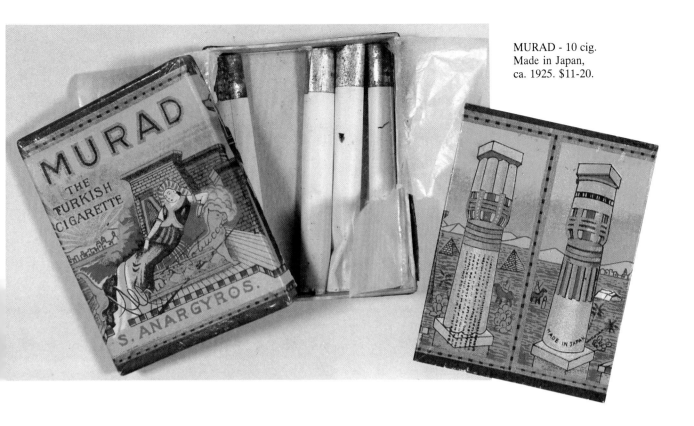

MURAD - 10 cig.
Made in Japan,
ca. 1925. $11-20.

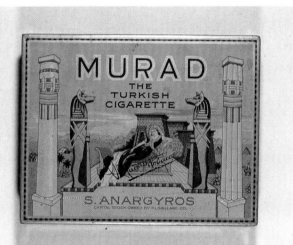

MURAD - 50 cig.
S. Anargyros, NY, USA, ca. 1930. Tin, $6-10.

MOSCOU - 10 cig.
Chapchal Fr, St. Petersburg,
Russia, ca. 1910. $21-40.

MURAD - 20 cig.
S. Anargyros, NY, USA, ca. 1925. $41-80.

MURATTI'S EGYPTIAN B. - 20 cig.
Muratti & Sons, London, UK, ca. 1930. $21-40.

MURATTI'S ARISTON - 20 cig.
B. Muratti & Sos, London, UK,
ca. 1930. Tin, $6-10.

Muratti's After Lunch - 20 cig.
B. Muratti & Sons, Manchester, UK,
ca. 1910. Tin, $41-80.

MURATTI'S AFTER LUNCH - 20 cig.
B. Muratti & Sons, London,
UK, ca. 1925. Tin, $41-80.

MURATTI GENTRY - 20 cig.
B. Muratti, Berlin, Germany
ca. 1935. $11-20.

MYRTLE GROVE - 100 cig.
Taddy & Co., London,
UK, ca. 1900. Tin, $41-80.

MYRTLE GROVE - 10 cig.
Taddy & Co., London,
UK, ca. 1970. $6-10.

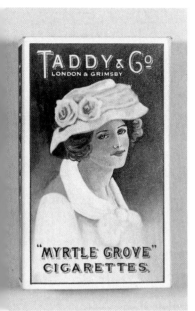

NAZIR - 20 cig.
Salonica Cig. Co., Alexandria,
Egypt, ca. 1935. $11-20.

MYRTLE GROVE - 10 cig.
Taddy & Co. London, UK,
ca. 1970. $6-10.

NATURAL LIGHTS - 20 cig.
Nat Sherman, New York, NY,
USA, ca. 1975. $6-10.

NAVY CLUB - 10 cig.
L. & J. Fabian, London, UK,
ca. 1950. $1-5.

NEPTUNE - 10 cig.
Hignett Bros & Co.,
UK, ca. 1925. $11-20.

NELISTA - 50 cig.
W.D. & H.O. Wills, Bristol - UK - 1940 ca. - $ 11 - 20

NELISTA - 50 cig.
W.D. & H.O. Wills, Bristol, UK, ca. 1930. $6-10.

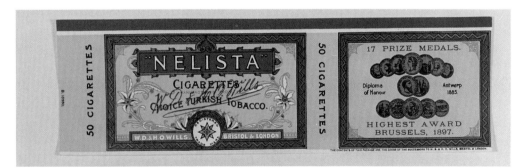

NELISTA - 50 cig.
W.D. & H.O. Wills, Bristol,
UK, ca. 1930. $6-10.

NELISTA - 50 cig.
W.D. & H.O. Wills, Bristol, UK, ca. 1940. $11-20.

NESHER - 20 cig.
Made in Israel,
ca. 1965. $1-5.

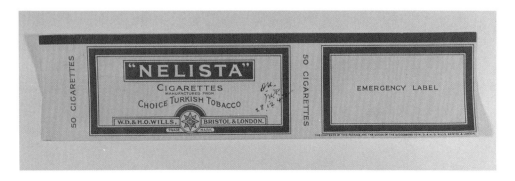

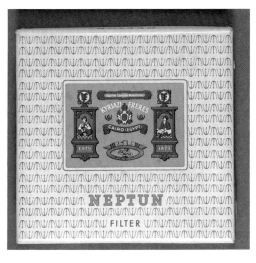

NEPTUN - 20 cig.
Kyriazi Freres,
Switzerland, ca. 1970. $1-5.

NELSON - 20 cig.
Israel Cig. Co., Tel Aviv,
Israel, ca. 1960. $1-5.

NEW YORKER - 20 cig.
Banju Mukti Cig. Factory,
Indonesia, ca. 1965. $1-5.

NEW YORK CITY LIGHTS - 10 cig.
N. Sherman, New York, USA,
ca. 1990. $1-5.

NEW YORK - 10 cig.
BAT Co., Holland,
ca. 1940. $6-10.

NEWPORT - 20 cig.
P. Lorillard, NC, USA, ca. 1965. $6-10.

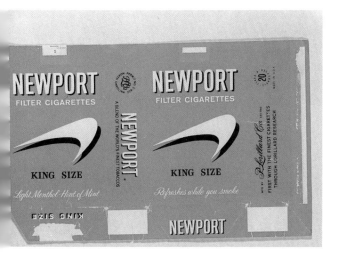

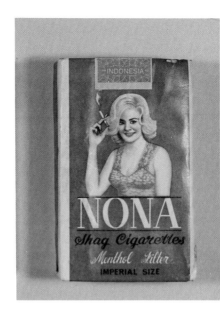

NIL - 50 cig.
Austria Tabak, Munich, Germany,
ca. 1965. Tin, $6-10.

NONA - 20 cig.
P.T. Soehoko, Surakarta, Indonesia
ca. 1980. $1-5.

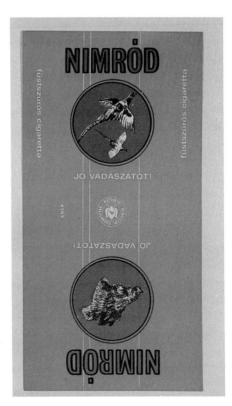

NIGHT CLUB - 50 cig.
Job, Switzerland, ca. 1965. Tin, $6-10.

NIMROD - 20 cig.
Magyar dohaniypar,
Hungary, ca. 1970. $1-5.

NISSAN - 10 cig.
Made in Japan,
ca. 1965. $1-5.

NORTH POLE - 3 cig.
Philip Morris Inc, Richmond, VA,
Switzerland, ca. 1970. $1-5.

NORFOLK - 10 cig.
Chr. Augustinus, Copenhagen,
Denmark, ca. 1955. $1-5.

NORTH STATE - 20 cig.
Brown & Williamson, Louisville, KY,
Holland, ca. 1975. $1-5.

NORTH STATE - 50 cig.
B & W, Louisville, KY,
USA, ca. 1960. Tin, $11-20.

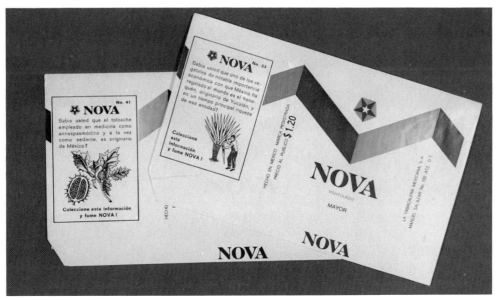

NOVA - 20 cig.
La Tabacalera Mexicana Sa,
Mexico, ca. 1970. $1-5.

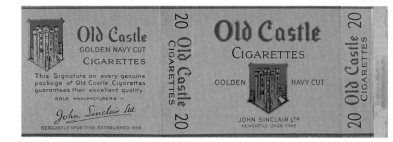

OLD CASTLE - 20 cig.
J. Sinclair Ltd., New Castle, UK, ca. 1950. $1-5.

NOVAS PLANETA - 20 cig.
TFK, Leningrad, USSR,
ca. 1960. $6-10.

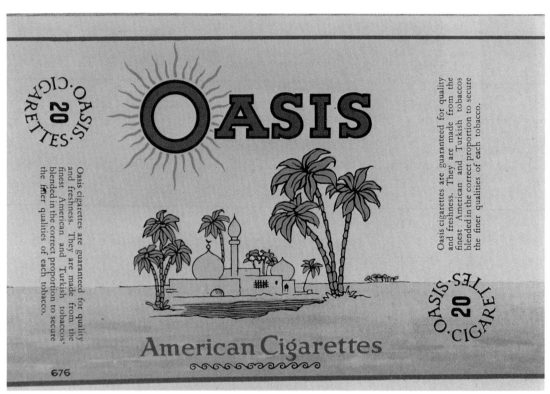

OASIS - 20 cig.
Made in Holland,
ca. 1970. $1-5.

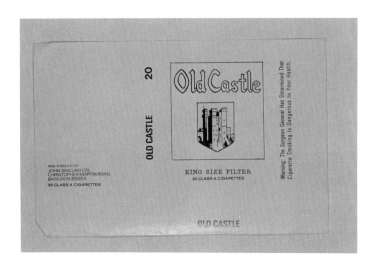

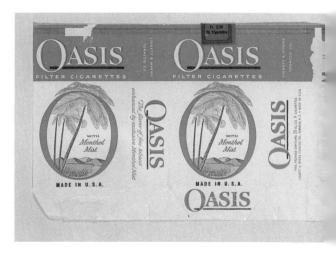

OLD CASTLE - 20 cig.
J. Sinclair Ltd., Basildon, UK, ca. 1965. $6-10.

OASIS - 20 cig.
L & M Tob. Co., Durham, NC, USA, ca. 1950. $1-5.

OLD GOLD - 20 cig.
P. Lorillard, KY, USA,
ca. 1940. $11-20.

OLD SHIPS - 10 cig.
The Dominion Tob. Co., UK, ca. 1930. $11-20.

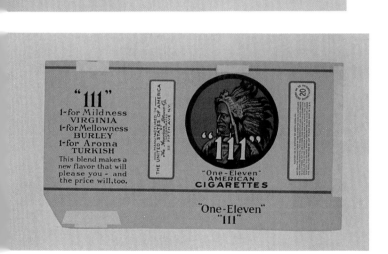

OLD GOLD FILTER - 20 cig.
P. Lorillard, KY,
USA, ca. 1950. $11-20.

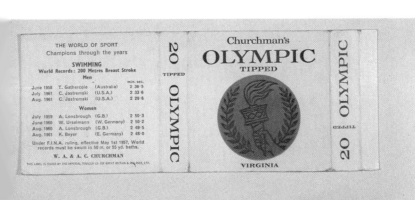

ONE-ELEVEN - 20 cig.
American Tob. Co., Fact. No. 30, NC, USA
ca. 1935. $21-40.

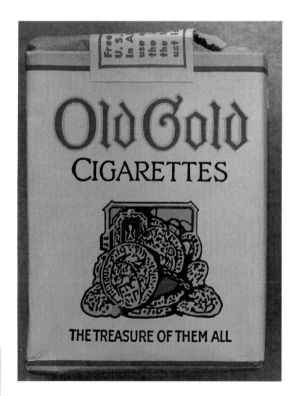

OLD GOLD - 20 cig.
Lorillard Co.,
USA, ca. 1944. $6-10.

OLYMPIC - 20 cig.
W.A. & A.C. Churchman, Ipswich, UK,
ca. 1962. $21-40.

OMAR - 100 cig.
Made in USA,
ca. 1940. Tin, $21-40.

OVERSEAS - 10 cig.
C. Colombos, Malta,
ca. 1920. Tin, $11-20.

OLD JUDGE
Goodwin & Co., New York, NY,
USA, ca. 1890. $21-40.

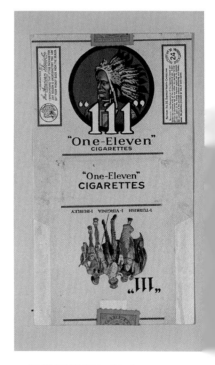

ONE-ELEVEN - 20 cig.
The American Tob. Co., USA
ca. 1935. $6-10.

OPERA - 25 cig.
Magyar Dohaniypar, Hungary, ca. 1970. $1-5.

ORIENTAL - 20 cig.
Sudan SA, Sao Paulo,
Brazil, ca. 1980. $1-5.

ORIENTAL - 20 cig.
Sudan SA, Sao Paulo,
Brazil, ca. 1970. $1-5.

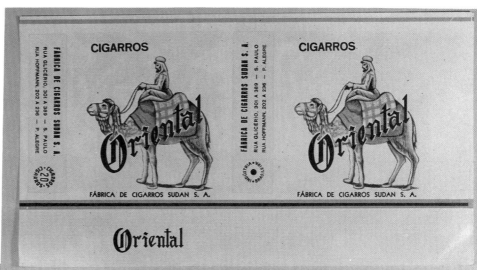

ORIENTALI - 20 cig.
Monopolio dei Tabacchi, Rome, Italy,
ca. 1930. $21-40.

PACO RABANNE - 20 cig.
Made in Switzerland,
ca. 1985. $1-5.

PALL MALL VIRGINIA - 20 cig.
Rothman's of Pall Mall, UK, ca. 1960. $1-5.

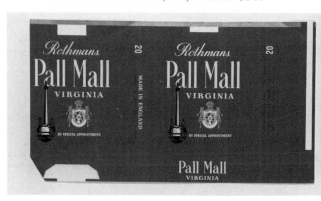

PALL MALL - 20 cig.
B.A.T. England, UK,
ca. 1975 ca. $1-5.

PANAMERICAN - 20 cig.
National Tob. Co., Newark, NJ, USA,
ca. 1955. $6-10.

PARIS - 20 cig.
A. Tabaqueria, Portugal
ca. 1970. $1-5.

PARIS - 20 cig.
Tabaqueira EP, Portugal, ca. 1975. $1-5.

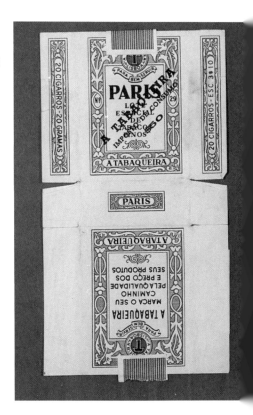

PALL MALL - 50 cig.
Rothman's Ltd., London,
UK, ca. 1930. Tin, $11-20.

PARACHUTE - 10 cig.
Made in Malta, ca. 1920. $6-10.

PALL MALL - 5 cig.
The American Tob. Co., Durham, NC,
USA, ca. 1965. $1-5.

PARISIENNES SUPER - 3 cig.
FJ Burrus, Boncourt,
Switzerland,
ca. 1965. $1-5.

PARISIENNES SUPER - 3 cig.
FJ Burrus, Boncourt, Switzerland
ca. 1965. $1-5.

PARLIAMENT - 20 cig.
Benson & Hedges, NY, USA,
ca. 1955. $11-20.

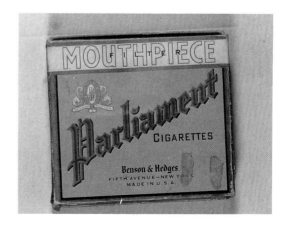

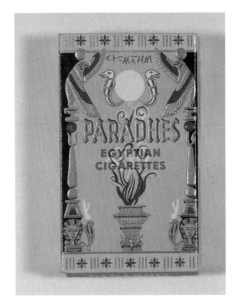

PARADHES - 10 cig.
Made in Malta,
ca. 1920. $6-10.

PARLIAMENT 100's - 5 cig.
Benson & Hedges, Richmond, VA,
USA, ca. 1975. $1-5.

PASHA' - 10 cig.
Wills, Bristol, UK,
ca. 1935. $11-20.

PATRIOTAS - 20 cig.
Urrutia y Solari, Chile,
ca. 1890. $11-20.

PASSING SHOW - 10 cig.
Carreras Ltd., London, UK,
ca. 1950. $1-5.

PASSING CLOUDS - 50 cig.
W. D. & H. O. Wills, Bristol, UK, ca. 1935. Tin, $21-40.

PATENT - 25 cig.
Wendt, Bremen,
Germany, ca. 1935. $6-10.

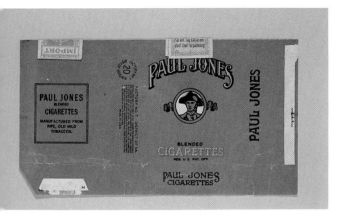

PAUL JONES - 20 cig.
Fact. No. 7, VA, USA,
ca. 1935. $21-40.

PAUL REVERE EXTRA - 20 cig.
American Cig. Co.,
Holland, ca. 1975. $1-5.

PAUL REVERE - 20 cig.
Rembrandt Tob. Corp., Zurich,
USA, ca. 1970. $1-5.

PAUL REVERE - 20 cig.
American Cig. Co., USA,
ca. 1970. $1-5.

PEACE - 50 cig.
Japan Tob. Corp., Japan,
ca. 1965. Tin, $11-20.

PEACE - 10 cig.
Japan Monopoly, Japan,
ca. 1964. $6-10.

PEACE - 10 cig.
Japan Monopoly, Japan
ca. 1965. $6-10.

PEACHEY - 20 cig.
Scotten Dillon Co., Detroit, MI, USA,
ca. 1930. $21-40.

PEACE - 10 cig.
Japan Monopoly, Japan
ca. 1964. $1-5.

PELLA LUXE - 20 cig.
Pella, Cavalla, Greece
ca. 1930. Tin, $11-20.

PERSI FRERES - 100 cig.
Persi Freres, Athens, Greece
ca. 1920. Tin, $11-20.

PERA - 20 cig.
C. Colombos, Ltd., Malta,
ca. 1915. $6-10.

PEER EXPORT - 3 cig.
Kristinus, Germany,
ca. 1960. $1-5.

PEERAGE - 20 cig.
Murray & Sons, Belfast, UK, ca. 1950. $6-10.

PERFECTOS No. 2 - 25 cig.
J. Player, Nottingham,
UK, ca. 1930. $11-20.

PEONY - 10 cig.
J.Mc. Kinnel, Edinburgh,
UK, ca. 1950. $6-10.

PERFECTOS FINOS - 25 cig.
J. Player, Nottingham, UK, ca. 1950. $11-20.

PERFECTOS FINOS - 50 cig.
J. Player, Nottingham, UK,
ca. 1950. $6-10.

PHENIX - 25 cig.
N. Gianaclis, Cairo,
Egypt, ca. 1935. Tin, $41-80.

PHILIP MORRIS - 3 cig.
Philip Morris & Co. Ltd. Inc.,
USA, ca. 1935. $11-20.

PENINSULARES - 20 cig.
Tabacalera Sa, Spain, ca. 1960. $1-5.

PHILIP MORRIS MULTIFILTER - 3 cig.
U.L. of Philip Morris Inc., NY,
Switzerland, ca. 1965. $1-5.

PHILTRES - 20 cig.
Seita, France,
ca. 1980. $1-5.

PHILIP MORRIS KING SIZE - 4 cig.
Philip Morris Inc., New York, NY, USA, ca. 1960. $6-10.

PICAYUNE - 20 cig.
Liggett Group, Durham, NC, USA,
ca. 1965. $6-10.

PICCADILLY CROSS CUT - 20 cig.
D. Ritchie & Co., Montreal, Canada,
ca. 1890. $21-40.

PIERRE CARDIN - 20 cig.
F.J. Burrus, Boncourt,
Switzerland, ca. 1985. $1-5.

PILOTO - 10 cig.
Cert. A 83 Verde, Buenos Aires, Argentina, ca. 1950. $1-5.

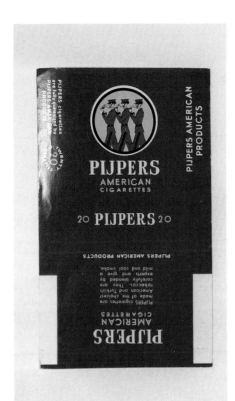

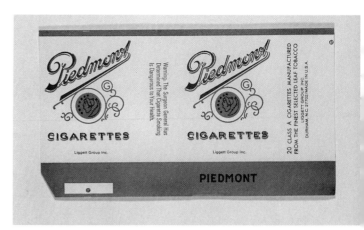

PIEDMONT - 20 cig.
Liggett Group, Durham, NC, USA, ca. 1970. $6-10.

PIJPERS - 20 cig.
Pijpers American Products,
Holland, ca. 1950. $1-5.

PICCADILLY JUNIORS - 10 cig.
Carreras Ltd., London, UK,
ca. 1955-ca. $1-5.

PINA FRANCIA - 30 cig.
Bataan Cig. & Cig. Fact., Quezon City,
Philippines, ca. 1965. $1-5.

PINAY - 30 cig.
La Campana Fabrica de Tabacos Inc.,
Philippines, ca. 1965. $6-10.

PIELROJA - 20 cig.
Cia Colombiana de Tabacos SA,
Colombia, ca. 1975. $1-5.

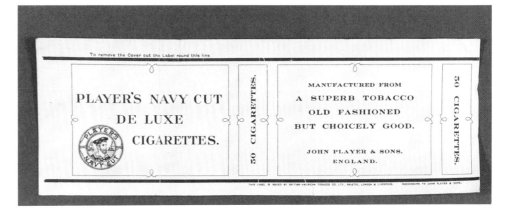

PIRATE - 10 cig.
W.D. & H.O. Wills, Bristol,
UK, ca. 1935. $1-5.

PIRATE - 50 cig.
W.D. & H.O. Wills, Bristol, UK, ca. 1942. $6-10.

PLAYER'S NAVY CUT DE LUXE - 50 cig.
J. Player, Nottingham, UK,
ca. 1930. $6-10.

PLANE - 50 cig.
Amalgamated Tob. Corp., London,
UK, ca. 1965. Tin, $6-10.

PIRATE - 10 cig.
W.D. & H.O. Wills, Bristol,
UK, ca. 1940. $6-10.

PLANET - 20 cig.
Courtaulds, London, UK,
ca. 1965. $6-10.

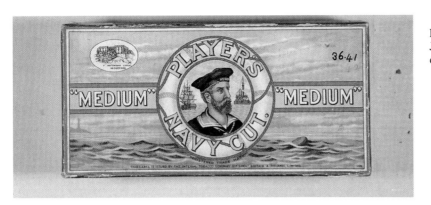

PLAYER'S NAVY CUT - 50 cig.
J. Player, Nottingham, UK,
ca. 1940. $11-20.

PLAYER'S NAVY CUT MILD - 50 cig.
Imperial Tob. Co., Montreal, Canada, ca. 1965. Tin, $6-10.

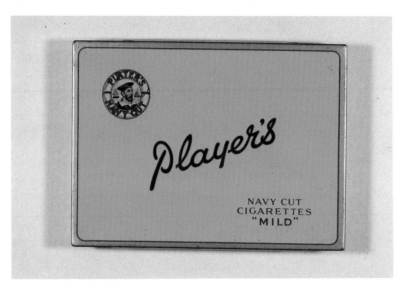

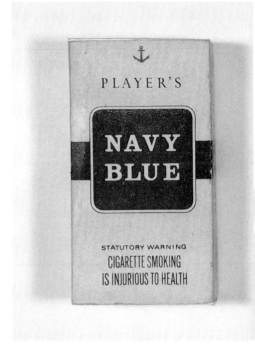

PLAYER'S Navy Blue - 10 cig.
Made in India,
ca. 1975. $1-5.

PLAYER'S FILTER TIP - 50 cig.
J. Player, Nottingham, UK, ca. 1940. $6-10.

PLAYER'S MEDIUM - 50 cig.
J. Player, Nottingham, UK, ca. 1940. $6-10.

PLAYER'S MEDIUM - 10 cig.
J. Player, Nottingham, UK,
ca. 1943. $6-10.

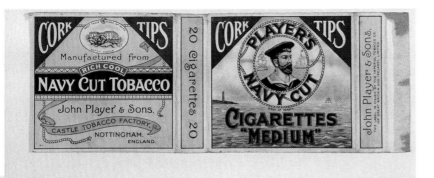

PLAYER'S CORK TIPS - 20 cig.
J. Player, Nottingham, UK,
ca. 1935. $6-10.

PLAYER'S NAVY CUT - 100 cig.
J. Player, Nottingham, UK,
ca. 1953. Tin, $21-40.
Coronation of Queen Elizabeth II.

PLAYER'S NAVY CUT - 50 cig.
J. Player, Nottingham,
UK, ca. 1935. $11-20.

PLAYER'S GOLD LEAF - 50 cig.
Player, UK, ca. 1930. $6-10.

PLAYER'S NAVY CUT - 20 cig.
J. Player, Nottingham, UK,
ca. 1950. $1-5.

PLAYER'S NAVY CUT - 50 cig.
Imperial Ltd., Canada,
ca. 1950. Tin, $11-20.

PLAYER'S MEDIUM - 60 cig.
J. Player, Nottingham, UK, ca. 1940. $11-20.

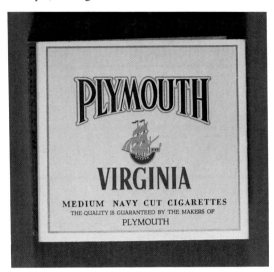

PLYMOUTH - 20 cig.
A. Batschari Cig. Fact., The Hague,
Holland, ca. 1960. $1-5.

PREMIER'S NAVY CUT - 20 cig.
Curzon Tob. Co., Montreal,
Canada, ca. 1955. $6-10.

POLO - 20 cig.
Pakistan Tob. Co. Ltd.,
Pakistan, ca. 1970. $1-5.

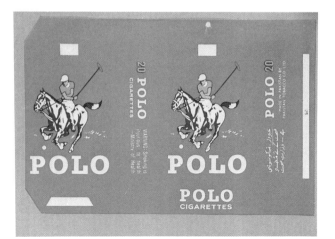

PLAZA - 10 cig.
Made in Holland,
ca. 1950. $6-10.

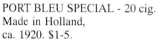

PORT BLEU SPECIAL - 20 cig.
Made in Holland,
ca. 1920. $1-5.

PORT ROYAL - 20 cig.
National Leaf Tob. Corp., NY, USA, ca. 1935. $11-20.

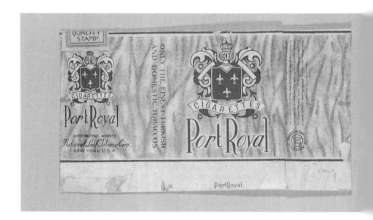

POWHATTAN - 10 cig.
American Tob. Co. A/S, Denmark, ca. 1960. $1-5.

PRIMÉROS - 20 cig.
Fabriquè en Suisse,
Switzerland, ca. 1980. $1-5.

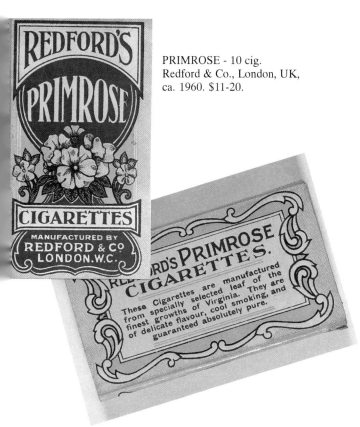

PRIMROSE - 10 cig.
Redford & Co., London, UK,
ca. 1960. $11-20.

PORTUGUES SUAVE - 20 cig.
A. Tabaqueira, Lisbon,
Portugal, ca. 1950. $6-10.

PRIZE CROP - 50 cig.
S. Mitchell & Sons, Glasgow,
UK, ca. 1930. $6-10.

PRIZE LEAF - 20 cig.
Redford & Co., London,
UK, ca. 1930. $6-10.

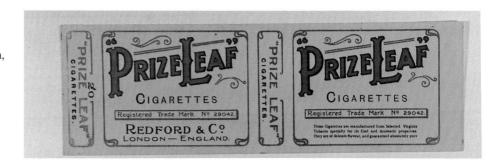

PRINCE DE MONACO - 50 cig.
Ed. Laurens, Brussels,
Belgium, ca. 1930. Tin, $21-40.

PREMIER'S MEDIUM - 50 cig.
The Premier Tob. Manuf. Ltd., London, UK, ca. 1935. $6-10.

PRINCE - 20 cig.
Scandinavian Tob. Co., Denmark, ca. 1980. $1-5.

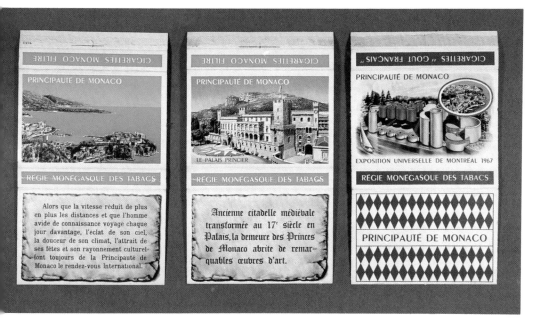

PRINCIPAUTE DE MONACO - 5 cig.
Regie Monegasque de Tabacs
Monaco, ca. 1970. $1-5 each.

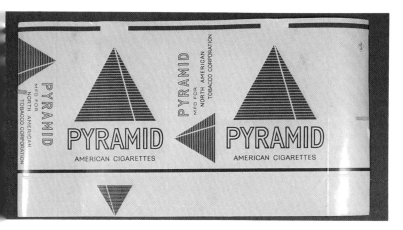

PYRAMID - 20 cig.
North American Tob. Corp., Hong Kong,
Hong Kong, ca. 1960. $1-5.

PROBINSYANA - 30 cig.
La Campana Fabrica de Tabacos Inc.,
Philippines, ca. 1960. $1-5.

PURITY SWEET
Pace & Sizer, Richmond, VA, USA
ca. 1890. $21-40.

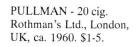

PULLMAN - 20 cig.
Rothman's Ltd., London,
UK, ca. 1960. $1-5.

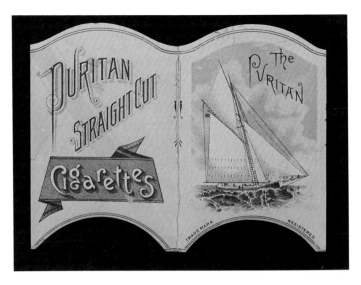

PURITAN STRAIGHT CUT
D. Ritchie & Co., Montreal,
Canada, ca. 1890. $21-40.

RAMI - 20 cig.
Salonica Cig. Co., Alexandria,
Egypt, ca. 1930. $21-40

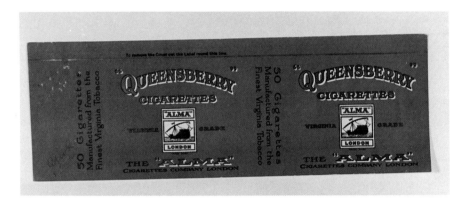

QUEENSBERRY - 50 cig.
The Alma Cig. Co., London,
UK, ca. 1930. $6-10.

QUEEN - 25 cig.
Nestor Gianaclis, Mainz,
Germany, ca. 1935. $21-40.

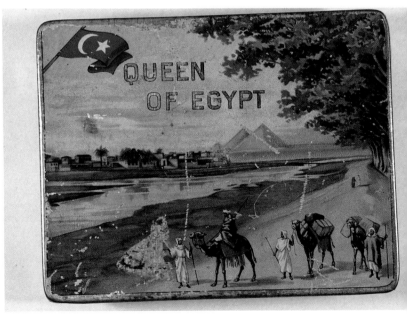

QUEEN OF EGYPT - 100 cig.
Przedcki Bros, Breslau, Germany
ca. 1910. Tin, $21-40.

QUEEN MARY - 10 cig.
Philips, UK, ca. 1930. $11-20.

RAINBOW - 20 cig.
Charles Fairmorn,
Germany, ca. 1985. $1-5.

RALEIGH - 20 cig.
B & W Tob. Corp., Louisville, KY,
USA, ca. 1945. $6-10.

RALEIGH - 20 cig.
B & W, Fact. No. 35, VA, USA
ca. 1943. $21-40
War Bonds an stamps.

REDFORD'S NAVY CUT - 10 cig.
Redford & Co., London
UK, ca. 1920. $11-20.

RAMINGA - 20 cig.
Manif. Zaratina Cig., Zara,
Italy, ca. 1930. $21-40.

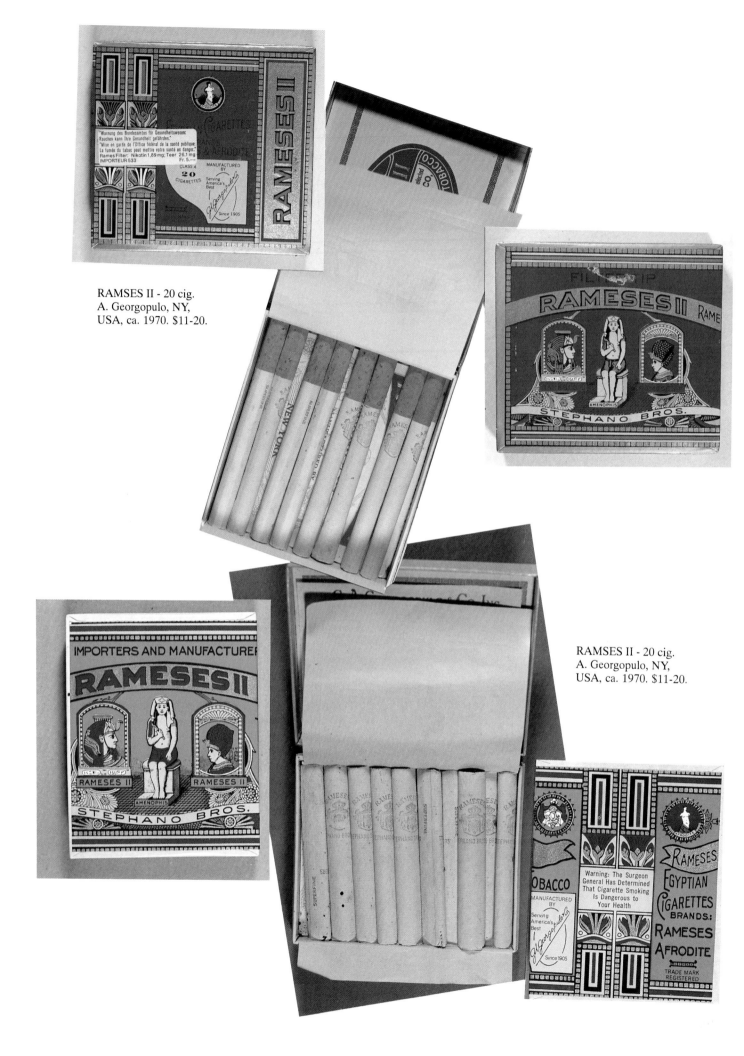

RAMSES II - 20 cig.
A. Georgopulo, NY,
USA, ca. 1970. $11-20.

RAMSES II - 20 cig.
A. Georgopulo, NY,
USA, ca. 1970. $11-20.

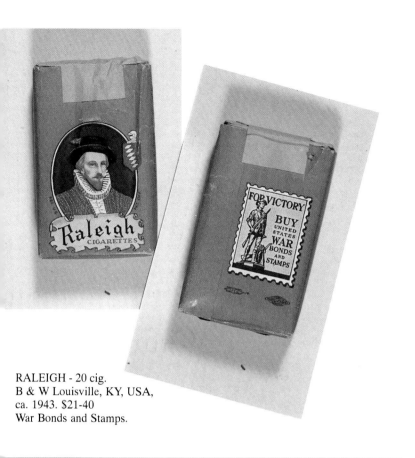

RALEIGH - 20 cig.
B & W Louisville, KY, USA,
ca. 1943. $21-40
War Bonds and Stamps.

RAMLY - 10 cig.
Fact. No. 456, MA,
USA, ca. 1901. $41-80.

RED & WHITE - 10 cig.
Premier Tob. Industries,
Pakistan, ca. 1970. $1-5.

RED & WHITE - 20 cig.
Marcovitch of Piccadilly, UK,
ca. 1955. $6-10.

RED BIRD - 10 cig.
Dominion Tob. Co. Ltd.,
India, ca. 1960. $1-5.

RED LAMP - 10 cig.
Peninsular Tob. Co. Ltd., Pakistan, ca. 1975. $1-5.

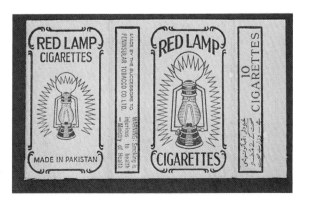

REGINA - 10 C.
Matossian, Le Caire, Egypt,
ca. 1937. $11-20.

REITSCHULE - 40 cig.
Cig. Constantin AG, Hannover, Germany,
ca. 1935. Tin, $11-20.

REINA VICTORIA - 10 cig.
Enrique Martinez, Buenos Aires,
Argentina, ca. 1930. $6-10.

REMBRANDT VAN RIJN - 20 cig.
Rembrandt Tob. Corp., Paarl,
South Africa, ca. 1980. $1-5.

RICHMOND GEM - 10 cig.
Ogden of Liverpool, UK, ca. 1935. $11-20.

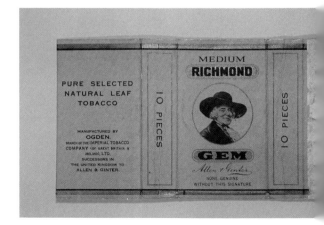

RICHMOND GEM - 100 cig.
The American Tob. Co, Richmond, VA,
USA, ca. 1910. Tin, $41-80.

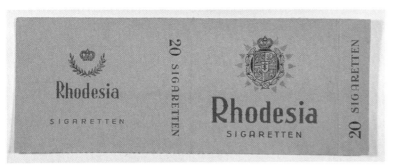

RHODESIA - 20 cig.
Made in Holland, ca. 1930. $6-10.

RIALTO - 20 cig.
C.ia de Cigarros Castelloes,
Argentina, ca. 1940. $1-5.

RENAULT - 10 cig.
Monopoli di Stato, Italy
ca. 1960. $11-20.

RICHMOND HIGH CLASS - 20 cig.
Richmond Cig. Co., Holland, ca. 1955. $1-5.

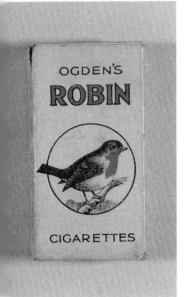

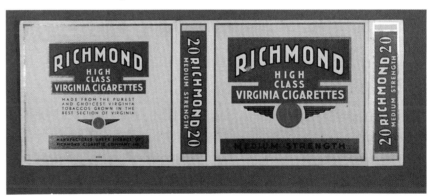

ROBIN - 10 cig.
Ogden's of Liverpool, UK,
ca. 1900. $1-5.

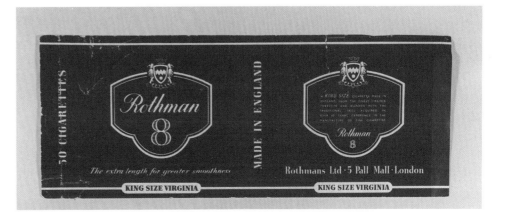

ROTHMAN 8 - 50 cig.
Rothman of Pall Mall, UK,
ca. 1930. $6-10.

ROOSTER - 20 cig.
Made in Kenya,
ca. 1965. $1-5.

ROBIN HOOD - 20 cig.
Hong Kong Tob. Co., ca. 1960. $6-10.

ROCKY - 10 cig.
C. Colombos Ltd., Malta,
ca. 1910. Tin, $21-40.

ROTHMANS VIRGINIA - 20 cig.
Rothmans of Pall Mall, UK,
ca. 1960. $1-5.

ROSA D'ORIENTE - 20 cig.
Monopoli di Stato, Italy,
ca. 1950. $21-40.

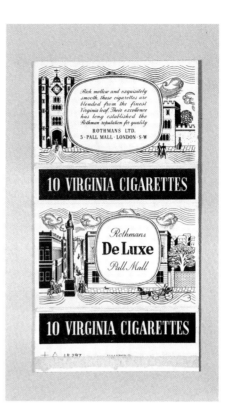

ROTHMAN'S DE LUXE - 10 cig.
Rothmans Ltd.,
London, UK,
ca. 1960. $6-10.

ROCKY MOUNTAINS - 20 cig.
Chr. Augustinus, Copenhagen, Denmark, ca. 1950. $1-5.

Rough Rider - 10 cig.
W.D. & H.O. Wills, Bristol,
UK, ca. 1950. $1-5.

ROVER - 20 cig.
Ardath Tob. Co., London,
UK, ca. 1950. $1-5.

ROTHMANS DE LUXE - 20 cig.
Rothmans of Pall Mall, London,
UK, ca. 1960. Tin, $6-10.

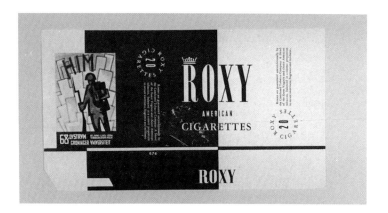

ROXY - 20 cig.
Combined Tob. Co.,
Holland, ca. 1968. $1-5.

ROYAL DERBY - 20 cig.
Ed. Laurens, Le Caire, Egypt, ca. 1925. Tin, $11-20.

ROYAL NAVY - 20 cig.
Made in Belgium, ca. 1935. $1-5.

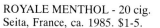

ROYALE MENTHOL - 20 cig.
Seita, France, ca. 1985. $1-5.

RUSSIAN BLEND - 20 cig.
B. Morris & Sons, London, UK,
ca. 1940. $6-10.

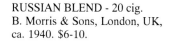

RUBY QUEEN - 50 cig.
W.D. & H.O. Wills, Bristol, UK,
ca. 1930. $6-10.

RUMMY - 100 cig.
Joseph Licari, Valetta,
Malta, ca. 1925. $6-10.

SALOME' - 10 cig.
Sato SA, Switzerland,
ca. 1925. $21-40.

SALEM - 4 cig.
R.J. Reynolds Tob. Co.,
USA, ca. 1965. $1-5.

SALONIQUE No. 1 - 20 cig.
La Ferme, Dresden, Germany,
ca. 1885. $21-40.

SALOMÈ - 10 cig.
Rosedor Cig. Co., NY,
USA, ca. 1925. $41-80.

SALEM AUSLESE - 25 cig.
Yenidze Cig. Gmbh, Dresden,
Germany, ca. 1925. $11-20.

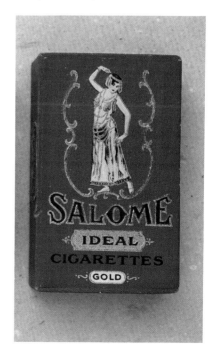

SAMBUL - 20 cig.
The Orient Cig. Co., Cairo,
Egypt, ca. 1925. $6-10.

SANTA FÉ - 20 cig.
Made in Holland,
ca. 1955. $6-10.

SATO - 10 cig.
Soc. Tabacs d'Orient, Switzerland,
ca. 1930. $11-20.

SAMSOUN EXTRA - 20 cig.
Matossian SA, Cairo, Egypt, ca. 1925. $6-10.

SANITAS No. 8 - 10 cig.
J. Przedecki, Breslau,
Germany, ca. 1913. $21-40.

SAMBA - 20 cig.
Tabacaria Londres SA, Rio de Janeiro,
Brazil, ca. 1965. $1-5.

SEA RAIDER - 10 cig.
The Osborne Tob. Co., London,
UK, ca. 1950. $6-10.

SARAJEVO - 20 cig.
Fabrika Duvana, Sarajevo,
Yugoslavia, ca. 1970. Tin, $6-10.

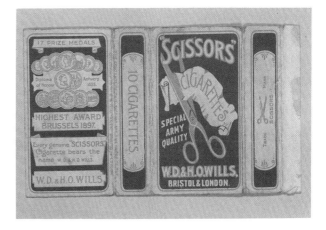

SCISSORS - 10 cig.
W.D. & H.O. Wills, Bristol, UK, ca. 1925. $11-20.

SARATOGA - 20 cig.
Philip Morris Inc., NY,
Switzerland, ca. 1970. $1-5.

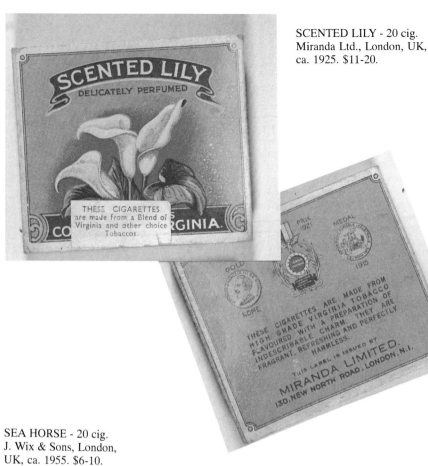

SCENTED LILY - 20 cig.
Miranda Ltd., London, UK,
ca. 1925. $11-20.

SHEFFIELD No. 5 - 20 cig.
Sheffield Tob. Work, NY,
USA, ca. 1950. $11-20.

SEA HORSE - 20 cig.
J. Wix & Sons, London,
UK, ca. 1955. $6-10.

SHOPRITE - 20 cig.
Permit no. 1, VA, USA,
ca. 1950. $11-20.

SENOUSSI No. 16 - 10 cig.
Reemtsma, Hamburg,
Germany, ca. 1920. Tin, $21-40.

SILON - 20 cig.
Lod Cig. Ltd., Lod,
Israel, ca. 1970. $1-5.

SENIOR SERVICE - 20 cig.
J.A. Pattreioeux, Manchester, USA, ca. 1950. $11-20.

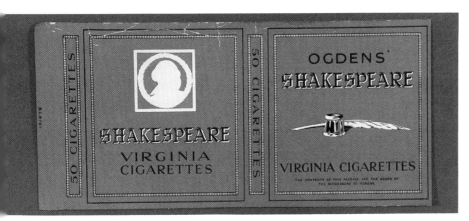

SHAKESPEARE - 50 cig.
Ogden of Liverpool, UK,
ca. 1930. $6-10.

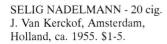

SELIG NADELMANN - 20 cig.
J. Van Kerckof, Amsterdam,
Holland, ca. 1955. $1-5.

SEPOY - 10 cig.
Peninsular Tob. Co., Monghyr,
India, ca. 1930. $6-10.

SEREIAS - 20 cig.
C.ia Portuguesa de Tabacos, Portugal, ca. 1955. $1-5.

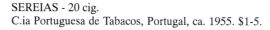

SERENISSIMA - 20 cig.
Man. Tab. Orientali, Zara, Italy,
ca. 1935. $21-40.

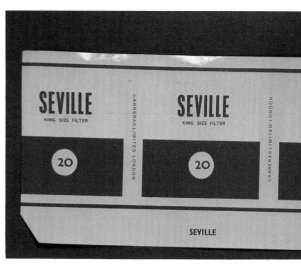

SEVILLE - 20 cig.
Carreras Ltd., London, UK,
ca. 1970. $1-5.

SENSATION - 20 cig.
P. Lorillard, NJ, USA,
ca. 1940. $11-20.

SHEPHEARD'S HOTEL - 20 cig.
Dimitrino & Co.,
Germany, ca. 1985. $1-5.

SHERMAN'S MCD - 20 cig.
Nat Sherman, New York, NY,
USA, ca. 1975. $6-10.

SIMON ARZT EXTRA MILD - 20 cig.
Simon Arzt Cig. Gmbh, Bonn, Germany,
ca. 1955. Tin, $6-10.

SHERMAN'S 164 - 10 cig.
Nat Sherman, New York, NY,
USA, ca. 1970. $6-10.

SINTANJIN - 20 cig.
Office of monopoly
South Korea
ca. 1965. $1-5.

SIMON ARZT No. 70 - 20 cig.
Simon Arzt, Alexandria, Egypt,
ca. 1960. Tin, $6-10.

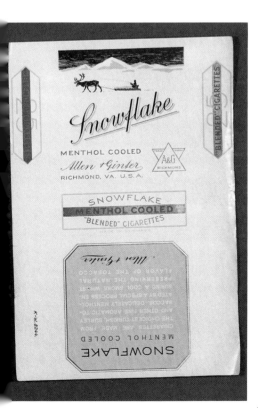

SNOWFLAKE - 25 cig.
Allen Ginter Richmond, Richmond, VA,
USA/Denmark, ca. 1960. $1-5.

SINTANJIN - 6 cig.
Office of Monopoly,
South Korea,
ca. 1965. $1-5.

SKI - 25 cig.
Goodlook & Co., Cairo, Egypt, ca. 1920. $11-20.

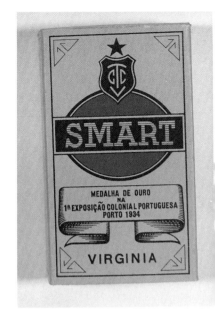

SMART - 10 cig.
C.ia dos Tabacos, S. Vincente,
Cabo Verde, ca. 1934. $6-10.

SMOKE CLOUD - 20 cig.
The Silk Leaf Tob. Co., UK, ca. 1940. $11-20.

SNAKE CHARMER - 20 cig.
Salmon & Gluckstein, London, UK,
ca. 1900. Tin, $80-200.

SOBRANIE STRAIGHT CUT - 20 cig.
Sobraine of London, UK,
ca. 1960. Tin, $6-10. For B.E.A.

SOBRANIE VIRGINIA n. 40
25 cig. - Sobranie of London
UK - 1965 ca. - $ 1 - 5 - Tin

SOVEREIGN - 20 cig.
The American Tob. Co., USA,
ca. 1945. $11-20.

SOBRANIE BLACK RUSSIAN - 12 cig.
Sobranie of London,
UK, ca. 1970. $1-5.

SOBRANIE MONTECARLO - 20 cig.
Sobranie of London,
UK, ca. 1970. $1-5.

SOEPIAH - 10 cig.
Larasati, Semarang,
Indonesia, ca. 1970. $1-5.

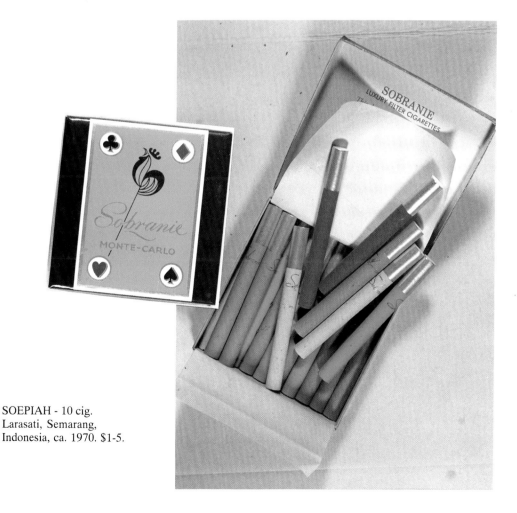

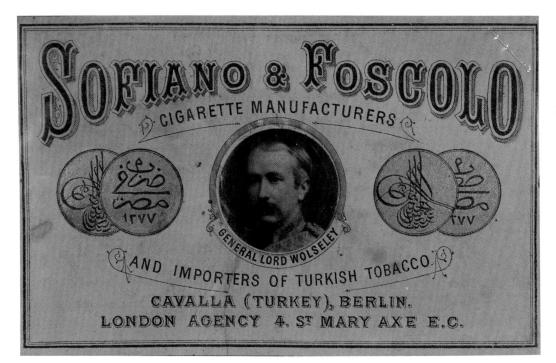

SOFIANO & FOSCOLO
Sofiano & Foscolo, London
UK, ca. 1910. $6-10.

SPINET - 20 cig.
R. & J. Hill, London,
UK, ca. 1930. Tin, $11-20.

SOUSSA EXTRA No. 6 - 20 cig.
Nicolas Soussa Fr., Cairo,
Egypt, ca. 1960. $6-10.

SPINET - 50 cig.
R. & J. Hill Ltd., London, UK,
ca. 1970. $1-5.

SPEEDWAY - 20 cig.
Mavros, Holland, ca. 1955. $1-5.

SOFIA - 20 cig.
Spou, Bulgaria,
ca. 1933. $11-20.

SPLENDO - 50 cig.
Ardath, London, UK,
ca. 1900. Tin, $41-80.

SPORTING - 20 cig.
C.ia Portuguesa de Tabacos, Portugal,
ca. 1955. $1-5.

SPORTSMEN - 20 cig.
Piccardo y C.ia Ltd.,
Buenos Aires, Argentina
ca. 1950. $1-5.

SPORTSMAN - 50 cig.
Ogden's of Liverpool, UK,
ca. 1930. $6-10.

SPRINGBOK - 20 cig.
The United Tob. Co., Capetown,
South Africa, ca. 1950. $6-10.

SPUD - 20 cig.
Philip Morris Inc., Richmond, VA,
USA, ca. 1955. $11-20.

SPLENDO - 20 cig.
Ardath Tob. Co., London, UK,
ca. 1925. $11-20.

SPUTNIK - 25 cig.
Yava, Moscow, USSR,
ca. 1965. $6-10.

SPRINGTIME - 20 cig.
Warwichs Factory Cig.,
Denmark, ca. 1960. $1-5.

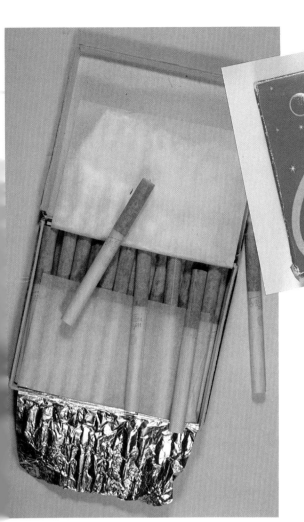

STAR - 10 cig.
Wills, Bristol, UK,
ca. 1930. $6-10.

SPUTNIK - 20 cig.
TFK, Leningrad,
USSR, ca. 1960. $6-10.

STAR - 20 cig.
Philip Morris Inc., Richmond, VA, USA, ca. 1985. $1-5.

STRAND - 10 cig.
W.D. & H.O. Wills, Bristol,
UK, ca. 1970. $1-5.

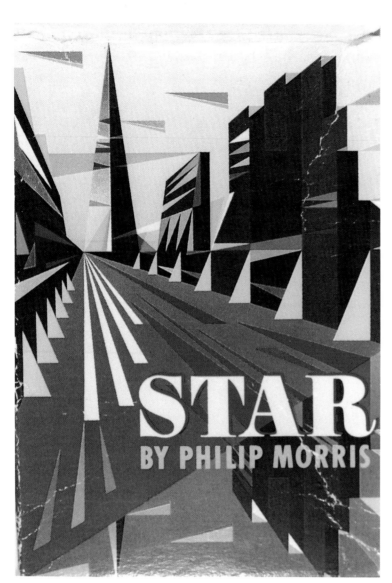

STAMBUL - 20 cig.
Hungarian Monopoly, Hungary, ca. 1928. $11-20.

STAR - 20 cig.
Philip Morris Inc.,
Richmond, VA,
USA, ca. 1985. $1-5.

STAR - 20 cig.
P. Morris, Richmond, VA,
USA, ca. 1980. $1-5.

STRAIGHT CUT CIGARETTES - 20 cig.
Ching & Co., Jersey, UK, ca. 1930. $11-20.

STARLET - 3 cig.
Made in Switzerland,
ca. 1960. $1-5.

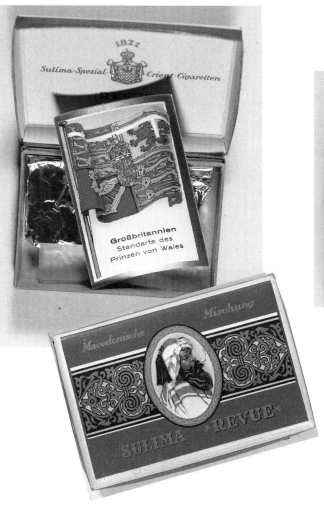

SULTAN EXPORT No. 12 - 25 cig.
Aurelia Cig. Gmbh, Dresden,
Germany, ca. 1920. Tin, $11-20.

SULIMA REVUE - 9 cig.
Sulima, Dresden,
Germany
ca. 1925. $11-20.

SUPERIORES AL CUADRADO - 20 cig.
Tabacalera SA, Spain, ca. 1950. $6-10.

SULIMA REVUE - 50 cig.
Sulima, Dresden, Germany
ca. 1900. Tin, $41-80.

SWEET CAPORAL - 20 cig.
Kinney Bros., Canada,
ca. 1943. $11-20. Aircraft series.

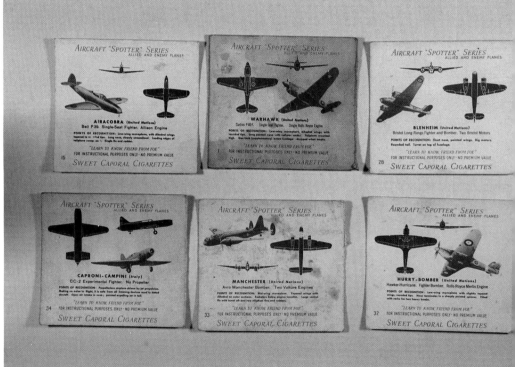

SWEET CAPORAL - 10 cig.
Kinney Bros., NY, USA, ca. 1891. $41-80.

SWEET CAPORAL - 20 cig.
The American Tob. Co., USA, ca. 1965. $6-10.

SWEET CAPS - 20 cig.
Made in Benelux,
Holland, ca. 1955. $6-10.

SWEET AFTON - 20 cig.
P.J. Carrols Ltd., Dundalk,
Ireland, ca. 1965. $1-5.

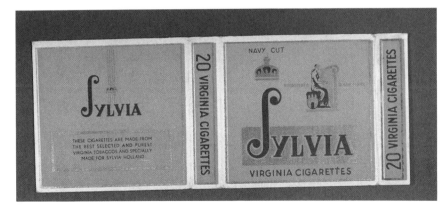

SYLVIA - 20 cig.
Sylvia Cigarettes, Holland
ca. 1950. $1-5.

SWEET SIXTEEN
D. Ritchie & Co., Montreal, Canada, ca. 1890. $21-40.

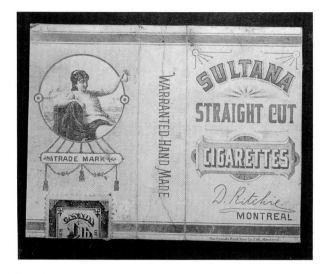

SULTANA STRAIGHT CUT - 10 cig.
D. Ritchie & Co., Montreal, Canada,
ca. 1890. $21-40.

TALK - 20 cig.
Made in Japan, ca. 1985. $1-5.

TANK - 20 cig.
Khyber Tob. Co., Pakistan, ca. 1970. $1-5.

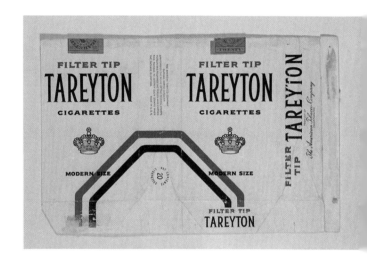

TAREYTON - 20 cig.
The American Tob. Co., NC
USA, ca. 1950. $6-10.

TATLER - 50 cig.
Arcadian Tob. Co. Ltd., Calcutta,
India, ca. 1930. $6-10.

TEAL - 50 cig.
BAT, UK,
ca. 1930. $6-10.

TEAL - 12 cig.
Ogden of Liverpool, UK,
ca. 1930. $11-20.

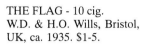

THE FLAG - 10 cig.
W.D. & H.O. Wills, Bristol,
UK, ca. 1935. $1-5.

TEOFANI'S KNOTS - 25 cig.
Teofani & Co. Ltd., UK,
ca. 1920. $11-20.

THE BALKAN SOBRAINE - 10 cig.
Sobranie of London, UK,
ca. 1985. $11-20.

THE DIAMOND
D. Ritchie & Co., Montreal, Canada,
ca. 1890. $21-40.

TEXAS - 10 cig.
Shrihesti, Kudus, Indonesia,
ca. 1965. $1-5.

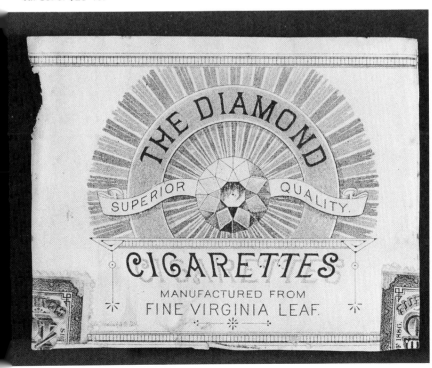

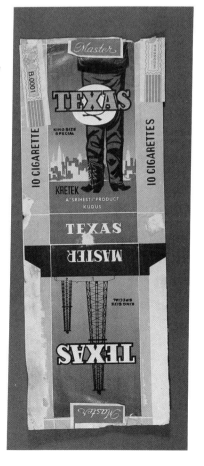

THE FLAG MAGNUMS - 50 cig.
W.D. & H.O. Wills, Bristol, UK,
ca. 1930. $6-10.

THE THREE CASTLES MEDIUM STRENGTH - 50 cig.
W.D. & H.O. Wills, Bristol, UK,
ca. 1930. $6-10

THE THREE CASTLES DIAMOND SIZE - 40 cig.
W.D. & H.O. Wills, Bristol
UK, ca. 1930. $6-10.

THE FLAG - 10 cig.
W.D. & H.O. Wills, Bristol, UK,
ca. 1930. $6-10.

THE GREYS - 20 cig.
Major Drapkin & Co, London, UK,
ca. 1930. $1-5.

TENNER - 10 cig.
W.A. & A.C. Churchman, Ipswich, UK, ca. 1935. $11-20.

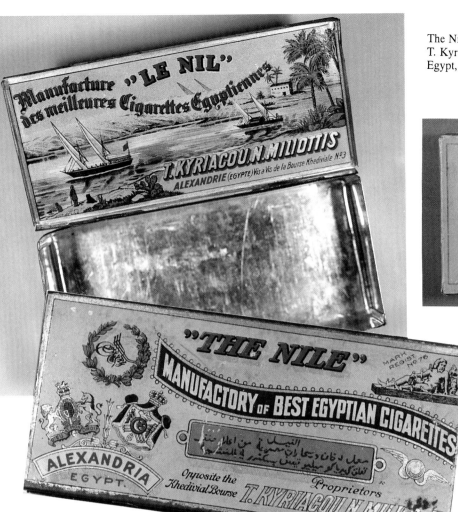

The Nile - 100 cig.
T. Kyriacou, N. Miliottis,
Egypt, ca. 1900. Tin, $21-40.

THE GREY'S SILK CUT - 25 cig.
G. Phillips, London, UK,
ca. 1950. $6-10.

THE THREE CASTLES IVORY TIPPED - 50 cig.
W.D. & H.O. Wills, Bristol, UK,
ca. 1930. $11-20.

THREE BELLS - 10 cig.
J. & F. Bell, Glasgow, UK,
ca. 1935. $6-10.

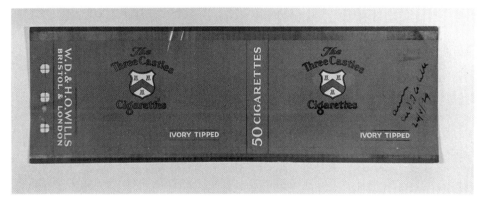

THE WALDORF ASTORIA - 20 cig.
Fact. No. 30, NC, USA,
ca. 1940. $11-20.

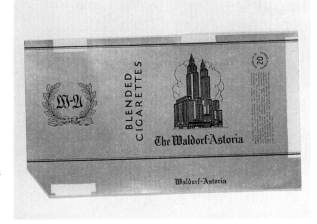

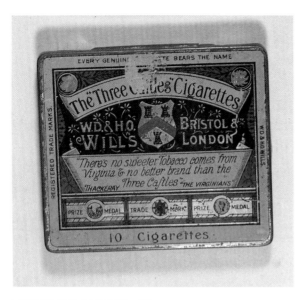

THE THREE CASTLES - 10 cig.
Wills, Bristol, UK,
ca. 1910. Tin, $21-40.

THE THREE CASTLES - 10 cig.
W.D. & H.O. Wills, Bristol,
UK, ca. 1935. $6-10.

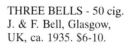

THREE BIRDS - 10 cig.
Gallaher Ltd., London,
UK, ca. 1940. $6-10.

THREE BELLS - 50 cig.
J. & F. Bell, Glasgow,
UK, ca. 1935. $6-10.

THE TOCCO'S - 10 cig.
Athanassacopulo B., Cairo,
Egypt, ca. 1930. $6-10

THREE LIONS - 20 cig.
J. Van Nelle, Rotterdam, Holland, ca. 1955. $1-5.

THREE GEESE - 15 cig.
Tradewell Tob. Co., UK,
ca. 1925. $11-20.

THREE CATS - 20 cig.
Carreras Ltd.,
London, UK,
ca. 1950. $6-10.

THREE STARS - 40 cig.
W.D. & H.O. Wills, Bristol, UK, ca. 1930. $6-10.

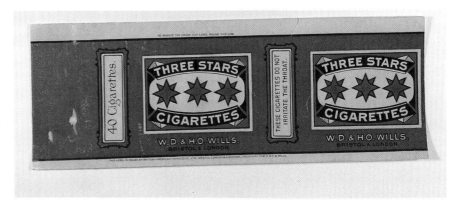

THREE HORSES - 50 cig.
King Tob. Co., Holland,
ca. 1955. $1-5.

TIGRA - 20 cig.
Cigarettes Tabalux, Belgium, ca. 1955. $1-5.

TIFFANY - 20 cig.
P. Morris, Germany,
ca. 1975. $41-80.

TIGRES - 20 cig.
La Libertad Sa, Mexico,
ca. 1960. $1-5.

TIGER - 20 cig.
P. Lorillard, NJ,
USA, ca. 1910. $41-80.

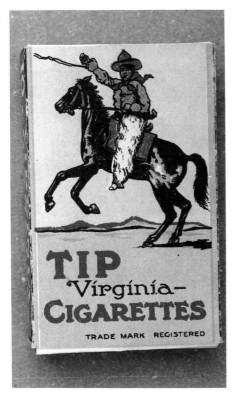

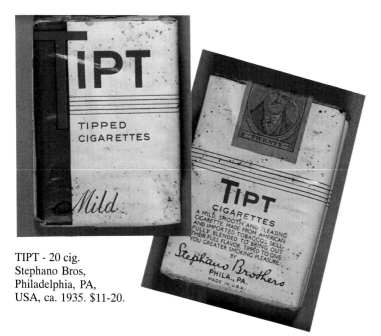

TIP - 10 cig.
Day's Tob. Co., London,
UK, ca. 1920. $11-20.

TIMES SQUARE - 20 cig.
National Leaf Tob. Co., Holland, ca. 1940. $1-5.

TIPT - 20 cig.
Stephano Bros,
Philadelphia, PA,
USA, ca. 1935. $11-20.

TORTOISESHELL - 20 cig.
Churchman, Ipswich, UK,
ca. 1910. Tin, $21-40.

TITINA - 30 cig.
Baatan Cigar & Cigarette Fact. Inc,
Philippines, ca. 1960. $1-5.

TORO - 10 cig.
Porto Rican American Tob. Co., Porto Rico, ca. 1900. $11-20.

TORCHLIGHT - 10 cig.
Gallaher Ltd., Singapore,
ca. 1955. $6-10.

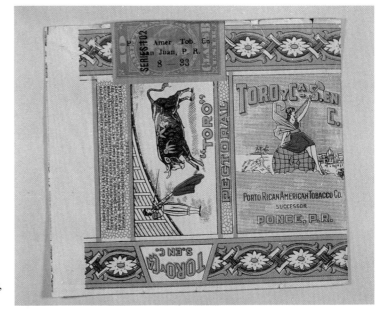

TORERO - 20 cig.
C.ia de Fumos, Santa Cruz,
Brazil, ca. 1970. $1-5

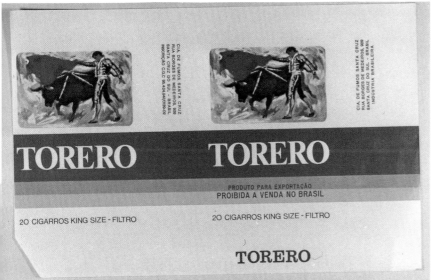

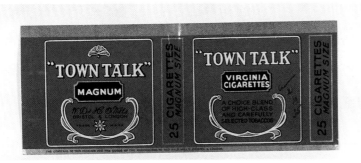

TRAWLER - 10 cig.
J.A. Pattreioeux, Manchester,
UK, ca. 1935. $11-20.

TOWN TALK - 25 cig.
W.D. & H.O. Wills, Bristol UK, ca. 1936. $6-10.

TOUTANKHAMON - 25 cig.
N. Gianaclis, Cairo, Egypt,
ca. 1930. Tin, $41-80.

TROYKA - 20 cig.
Fact. 392, Switzerland
ca. 1960. $1-5.

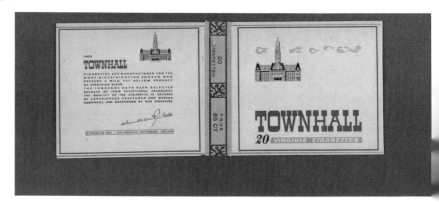

TOWNHALL - 20 cig.
J. Van Nelle NV, Rotterdam, Holland,
ca. 1960. $1-5.

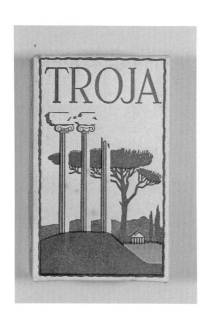

TROJA - 20 cig.
Svenska Tobac Monopolet, Sverige,
ca. 1950. $1-5.

TORTOISESHELL - 20 cig.
W.A. & A.C. Churchman, Ipswich, UK, ca. 1950. $6-1

TROPHY - 20 cig.
A. Broches & Co., Amsterdam,
Holland, ca. 1955. $1-5.

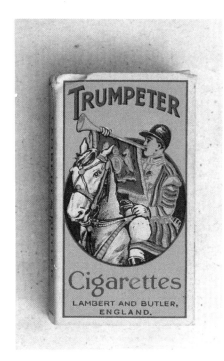

TRUMPETER - 10 cig.
Lambert & Butler, UK,
ca. 1930. $11-20.

TSAREVITCH - 5 cig.
Made in Switzerland,
ca. 1960. $1-5.

TRUSSARDI - 20 cig.
Austria Tabak, Austria,
ca. 1990. $1-5.

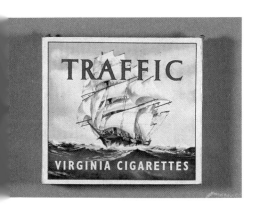

TRAFFIC - 20 cig.
The Combined Tob. Co.,
Holland, ca. 1940. $6-10.

TUFUMA - 10 cig.
A. Batschari, Neuchatel,
Switzerland, ca. 1935. $6-10.

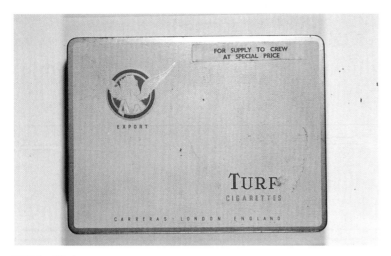

TURF - 50 cig.
A. Boguslavski, London,
UK, ca. 1900. $11-20.

TU-104 - 20 cig.
Made in Belgium, USSR,
ca. 1965. $1-5.

TURF - 50 cig.
Carreras Ltd., London, UK, ca. 1950. $11-20.

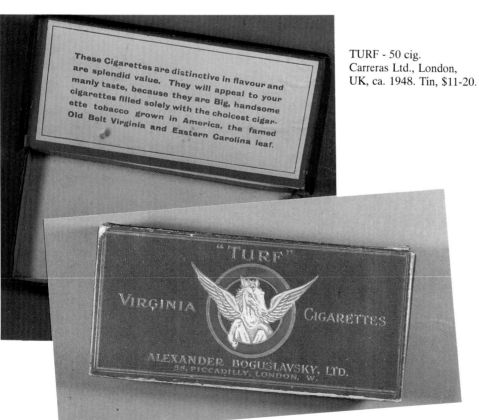

TURF - 50 cig.
Carreras Ltd., London,
UK, ca. 1948. Tin, $11-20.

TUTON - 10 cig.
PR Poohien, Semarang,
Indonesia, ca. 1970. $1-5.

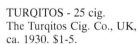

TWIGGY - 25 cig.
Made in Holland, ca. 1970. $1-5.

TURMAC BOUQUET - 20 cig.
Turmac, Zurich, Switzerland,
ca. 1930. $6-10.

TURQITOS - 25 cig.
The Turqitos Cig. Co., UK,
ca. 1930. $1-5.

TURMAC ORANGE - 25 cig.
Turkish Macedonian Tob., Zurich, Switzerland, ca. 1929. $11-20.

TURKISH BLEND - 20 cig.
B. Morris, London,
UK, ca. 1955. $6-10.

TURMAC ORANGE - 50 cig.
Turkish Macedonian Tob. Co., Zurich,
Switzerland, ca. 1930. Tin, $11-20.

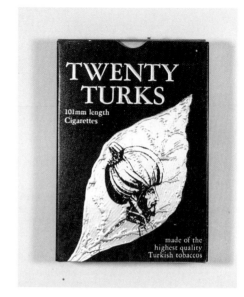

TWENTY TURKS - 20 cig.
Briki Tob. Co., Miami, FL,
USA, ca. 1965. $6-10.

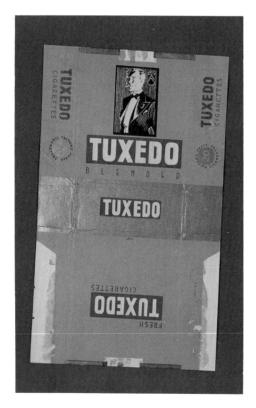

TUXEDO - 20 cig.
Made in Holland,
ca. 1940. $1-5.

TURMAC TASH-KA - 10 cig.
Turmac Sa, Zurich,
Switzerland, ca. 1930. $6-10.

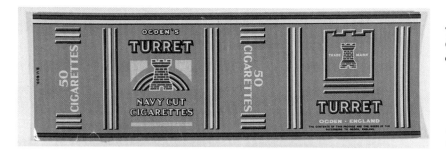

TURRET - 50 cig.
Ogden of Liverpool, UK,
ca. 1930. $6-10.

TWELVE O' CLOCK - 50 cig.
The Premier Tob. Manuf. Ltd., London,
UK, ca. 1930. $6-10.

TUXEDO - 20 cig.
American Tob. Co., USA,
ca. 1940. $11-20.

UNITED EMPIRE - 50 cig.
W.D. & H.O. Wills, Bristol,
UK, ca. 1930. $6-10.

URCA - 20 cig.
Sudan Sa, Sao Paulo, Brazil, ca. 1980. $1-5.

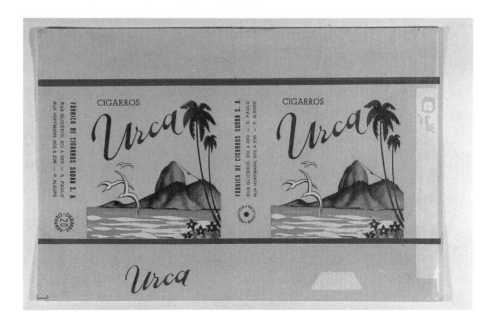

TWELVE O'CLOCK - 10 cig.
Silk Leaf Tob. Co., London,
UK, ca. 1950. $6-10.

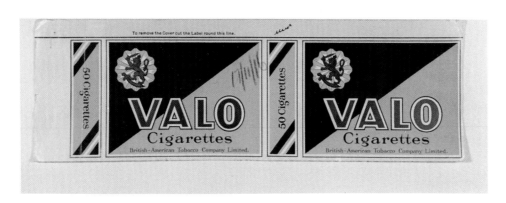

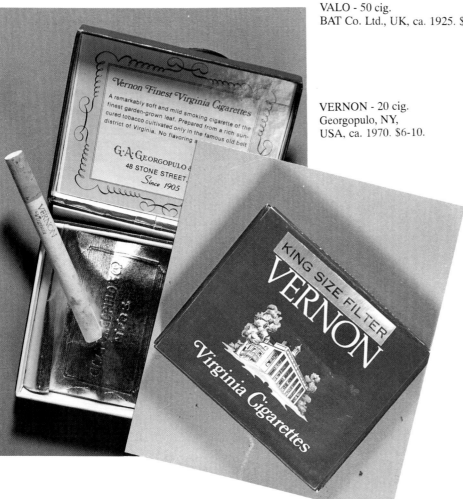

VALO - 50 cig.
BAT Co. Ltd., UK, ca. 1925. $6-10.

VERNON - 20 cig.
Georgopulo, NY,
USA, ca. 1970. $6-10.

VICEROY - 4 cig.
B & W. Tob. Corp., Louisville, KY,
USA, ca. 1960. $1-5.

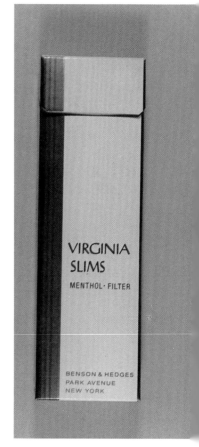

VIRGINIA SLIMS - 5 cig.
Benson & Hedges, New York,
USA, ca. 1980. $1-5.

VIRGINIA FILTRA - 10 cig.
Ed. Laurens, Geneva, Switzerland, ca. 1960. $1-5.

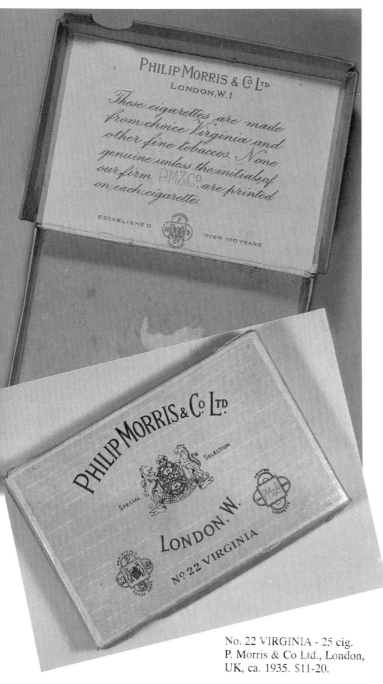

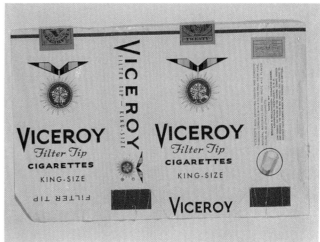

VICEROY - 20 cig.
B & W, Louisville, KY, USA, ca. 1955. $6-10.

VOGUE - 20 cig.
Made in USA,
ca. 1970. $1-5.

No. 22 VIRGINIA - 25 cig.
P. Morris & Co Ltd., London,
UK, ca. 1935. $11-20.

VOLGA - 25 cig.
Made in Belgium, ca. 1940. $1-5.

VOLVO - 20 cig.
Made in Holland,
ca. 1960. $1-5.

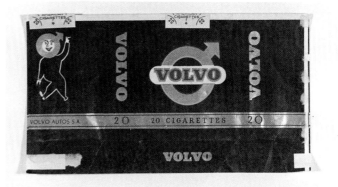

VULCAN - 20 cig.
Excel Tob. Co. Ltd., London, UK,
ca. 1935. $6-10.

WEIGHTS - 10 cig.
J. Player Nottingham, UK,
ca. 1944. $11-20.
Emergency packet.

WALDORF ASTORIA - 25 cig.
Waldorf Astoria, Germany, ca. 1929. Tin, $11-20.

WALLRUTH - 25 cig.
Wallruth Comp. Ag, Stuttgart,
Germany, ca. 1915. $11-20.

WASHINGTON - 20 cig.
Bejarano Bros.,
Tel Aviv, Israel,
ca. 1970. $1-5.

WALLSTREET - 20 cig.
Winchester Co., Holland,
ca. 1955. $1-5.

WARRIOR - 25 cig.
Made in Armenia, USSR,
ca. 1955. $6-10.

WATERFORD - 20 cig.
The American Tob. Co., USA,
ca. 1965. $11-20.

WALTER'S MEDIUM - 10 cig.
Walters Tob. Co., London, UK, ca. 1950. $1-5.

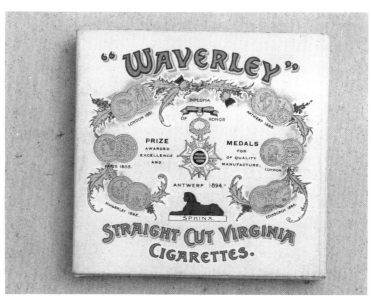

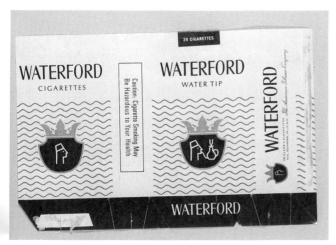

WAVERLEY - 10 cig.
Lambert & Butler, London, UK,
ca. 1940. $11-20.

WEINBERG'S SPECIAL
Weinberg, UK,
ca. 1920. $6-10.

WILD WOODBINE - 5 cig.
W.D. & HO.O. Wills, Bristol,
UK, ca. 1930. $6-10.

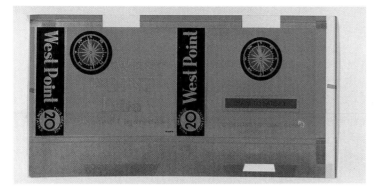

WEST POINT - 20 cig.
Cumberland Exp. Tob. Co., Holland, ca. 1955. $1-5.

WEST END - 20 cig.
Rothmans, London, UK, ca. 1950. $11-20.

WELLINGTON - 10 cig.
R. Faerce, Denmark, ca. 1960. $1-5.

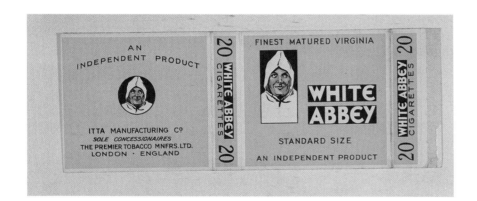

WHITE HORSE - 20 cig.
Rothman's of Pall Mall, UK,
ca. 1948. $6-10.

WHITE ABBEY - 20 cig.
Premier Tob. Ltd., London, UK,
ca. 1950. $6-10.

WESTMINSTER - 50 cig.
Westminster Tob. Co., London, UK,
ca. 1935 ca $6-10.

WHITE EAGLE - 20 cig.
Carreras Ltd., London,
UK, ca. 1960. $1-5.

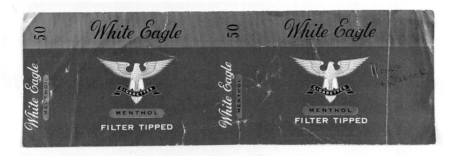

WINGS - 20 cig.
B & W, Louisville, KY,
USA, ca. 1960. $1-5.

WHITE EAGLE MENTHOL - 50 cig.
Carreras Ltd., London,
UK, ca. 1935. $6-10.

WINSTON - 4 cig.
R.J. Reynolds Tob. Co., Richmond, VA,
USA, ca. 1965. $6-10.

WHITE LINER - 20 cig.
Made in Denmark,
ca. 1955. $1-5.

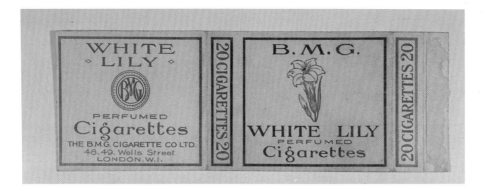

WHITE LILY - 20 cig.
The B.M.G. Cig. Co., London, UK, ca. 1930. $11-20.

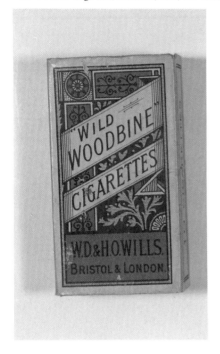

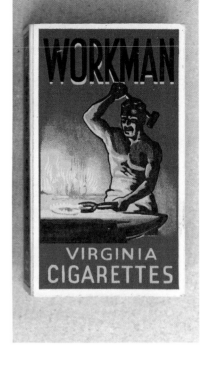

WORKMAN - 10 cig.
Made in Malta, ca. 1930. $1-5.

YUKON - 20 cig.
Larus Bros, Richmond, VA,
USA, ca. 1960. $6-10.

WILD WOODBINE - 10 cig.
W.D. & H.O. Wills, Bristol, UK,
ca. 1935. $1-5.

WHITE TOWN - 10 cig.
Made in Denmark,
ca. 1950. $1-5.

YOUR OWN - 20 cig.
J. Van Kerckhof, Amsterdam, Holland, ca. 1950. $1-5.

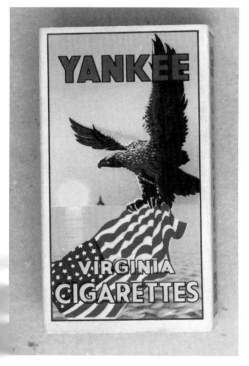

YANKEE - 10 cig.
Joseph Licari, Malta
ca. 1930. $1-5.

YVES SAINT LAURENT - 20 cig.
RJR Tob. Co. Winston-Salem, NC,
USA, ca. 1985. $1-5.

XCIRVIS - 10 cig.
Standard Tob. Co. Ltd., UK,
ca. 1920 ca $6-10.

YANKEE - 10 cig.
Made in Malta,
ca. 1920. $6-10.

YAMAHA-30 - 10 cig.
Made in Japan
Japan, ca. 1965. $1-5.

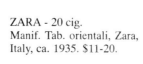

ZARA - 20 cig.
Manif. Tab. orientali, Zara,
Italy, ca. 1935. $11-20.